BOOK AB

by
Hilary Burkard
& Tom Burkard

Stories illustrated by
Ed McLachlan

First published 2004, Hilary Burkard
Second Edition (Revised) 2006, Hilary Burkard
Third Edition (Revised) 2013, Hilary Burkard

Copyright © Hilary Burkard 2013

All rights reserved. No part of this publication may be reproduced or transmitted in any form or by any means, electronic or mechanical, including photocopying, recording, or any information storage or retrieval system, without the written permission of the publisher.

ISBN: 978-1-905174-36-2

PUBLISHED BY HILARY BURKARD

DISTRIBUTED BY
SOUND FOUNDATIONS
www.soundfoundations.co.uk
sales@soundfoundations.co.uk
☎ 08448 708158 FAX 08448 708172

The Ground Rules	4
The Teaching Techniques	5
Decoding Power Pages	10
ee, ar, sh	12
er, th, ck	14
or, ch, qu	16
oy, ai, oa, ay, oi	18
air, eer, oar, ore	20
Final Consonant Blends	23
Fluency Reading	26
Initial Consonent Blends	40
Suffixes	61
-ing, -e, -all, -ly, -ed	62
Cloze Sentences	64
should, would, could, how, now, your	65
-es, -est, -ful, -less, -en, -y	68
very, many, any, one, done, none	70
-ck, -ke: The Silent 'e' Rule	73
want, watch, walk, water, wash, above, love	81
re-, be-, un-, ex-, pre-, dis-	86
-igh, -tch, -dge	90
Wordbuilding	92
ir, ur, -ce, -ge	97
cook, book, look, foot, good, took, what, when, which	100
aw, au	104
teach, real, eat, please, year, leave, meat, friend	120
out, found, our, loud, house, about, sure, sugar	147
ew, ue	152
Three Letter Blends	159
old, cold, hold, both, most, were, once, only	169

Introduction:

The **Sound Foundations** philosophy:

As a teacher, your objective is to get your pupil to make the maximum number of correct responses—*and* the fewest errors—in the available time. If you manage to do this, you can't go far wrong, no matter how you use our books.

The Ground Rules:

1. **Teach—don't test.** Whenever a child gets stuck, say the sounds for them or tell them the word. Do not force them to 'work it out for themselves'. You do not want to make reading into a struggle.

2. **Do not give ticks for a 'good try'.** Just practise it and go back to it the next day.

3. **Keep the lesson going at a cracking pace.** Do not let your pupil's attention wander.

4. **Daily lessons are essential.** You only need to find 10 minutes per day for each slow reader.

The Teaching Techniques:

1. **Using the flashcards**—oddly enough, this is the hardest part! If you did not grow up playing card games, just handling the cards can be tricky. Be sure you read the instructions carefully.

2. **Using the cursor**—This is quite easy to learn. The cursor trains the child to read from left to right, and it trains them to look at every letter in a word.

3. **The 'Flashback' technique**—After you have corrected an error, you must return to the same item again.

All this is explained on the following pages. Please read them carefully.

The Flashcards—it is not enough just to 'know' the letter-sounds. If the response is not instant and automatic, your pupil will not be able to concentrate on sounding out words. You must practise the flashcards *every* lesson while using **Fast Track**.

Before you start—There are two sets of flashcards. The first set is printed on green card—you will use them right from the beginning. Start introducing the second set, printed on blue card, after page 23.

Cut up the green flashcards along the lines printed on the back. It is important to cut them accurately—the cards are hard to handle if they are not exactly the same size.

Getting started—First, you must find out what letters your pupil already knows. Starting with the lowest-numbered cards, ask him what sound the letter makes. If he gives the letter name, say

"That's the *name* of the letter. But what *sound* does it make?"

Once the pupil has missed five in a row, it's best to stop. Put all of the letters he knows inside the front pocket of the book. Put all the rest in the pocket inside the back cover.

Daily revision—At the beginning of each lesson, always go through all of the flashcards in the front pocket. As the pupil gets each one right, place it in a pile in front of him.

If the pupil makes a mistake, use the **flashback technique:**
- Tell the pupil the right sound
- Ask him to repeat it
- Place the card behind the next one

When the card comes up again, he will almost certainly get it right. This way, you have converted an error into a success.

Shuffle the cards to mix up the order before you put them away.

Introducing a new sound—When you have finished the daily revision then, unless your pupil has made more than two errors, you should introduce a new sound.

Select the lowest-numbered card from the back pocket. Hold it up and say;

> "This card makes the sound *xx*. What sound?"

Make sure the pupil pronounces the sound correctly. If he has a speech defect, make sure that he pronounces it the same as he does in a word.

- Pick out three dissimilar flashcards that the pupil already knows. They should not sound or look like the letter you are introducing—for instance, you would never use the letter /t/ when introducing /d/, or use the letter /n/ when introducing /u/.

- Mix the new card in with the other three and practise them until perfect. If the pupil forgets the new card, use the "flashback" technique as described above.

The pupil may forget the new sound the next time you do your daily revision. However, by using the flashback technique, they almost always start getting it right in a day or two—*it really is that easy!*

When to stop using the flashcards—When the pupil can say the sounds quicker than you can flip the flashcards then, unless he has not reached the page introducing that sound in the book, you can stop practising those cards. The vowels and digraphs always take longer—you may still be using a few when you start **Dancing Bears C.**

Do not be tempted to stop using the flashcards too soon, thinking that the child already 'knows' the letters. Children must be able to respond instantly and automatically to the flashcards. Otherwise, they will have trouble blending. When they are trying to sound out c-a-t, they will forget the 'c' by the time they get to the 't'. You must "practise past the point of perfection." And no—your pupils will not get bored: children love getting it right!

Using the cursor—A cursor is a piece of card about the size of a business card with a small notch cut out of one corner. You must use the cursor at all times.

• When your pupil is sounding out a word, you can reveal one sound at a time. For example, the word shark has three sounds—*sh...ar...k.*

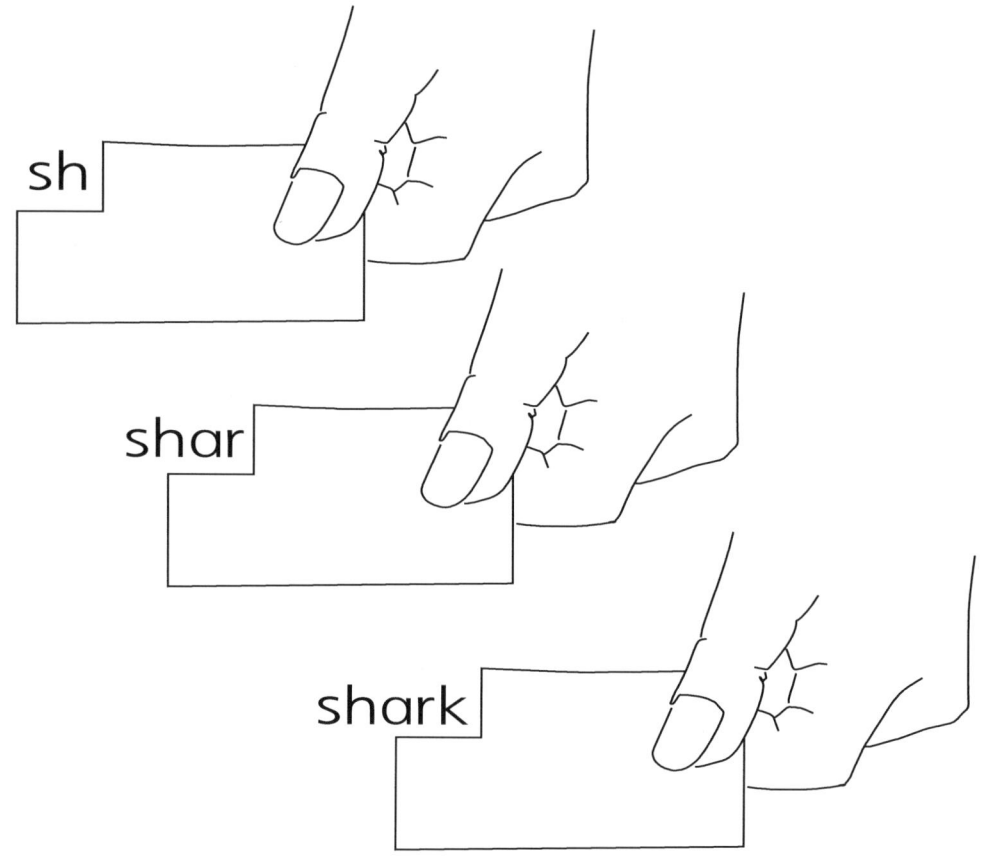

• When your pupil already knows a word, just move the cursor smoothly and quickly across the letters. Never sound out words if you do not need to.

• If your pupil makes a mistake, you can back up with the cursor and then sound out the word.

The cursor eliminates visual confusion. When children have been taught to read whole words, their eyes often jump all over the place, trying to scramble the letters to make a 'fit' with a word they know. If you use the cursor, it is highly unlikely that your pupil will need coloured overlays or tinted glasses.

The Flashback Technique—is used every time your pupil makes an error. If you go back to the instructions for using the flashcards, you will see that when your pupil has forgotten a sound, you tell him what it is and put it behind the next card. That way it comes up again while it is still fresh in his memory. This is an example of the **Flashback Technique**.

You will also use the **Flashback Technique** when your pupil is reading words. If your pupil fails to read the word:

- correct him,
- get him to repeat it,
- go on to the next item,
- go back to the one he just missed,
- when you have finished a line, go back again to any words missed,
- when you have finished the exercise for the day, go back over all words missed again.

This way, your pupil will usually earn his tick for the line the next day. (Remember—you never tick a line when the pupil gets it right on the second go—you must wait until the next lesson.)

The Teaching Environment—Always teach your pupil in a quiet room with no distractions. Do not let him bring toys or a mobile phone with him.

Always sit facing your pupil. It is very difficult to use the cursor sitting side-by-side. When you are facing your pupil it is easier to see when he is confused or getting tired. You can step in right away and show him what to do before he makes a mistake and loses confidence.

Fast Track

Decoding Power Pages:

These exercises are the 'secret ingredient' of **Fast Track**. All good readers can decode letters to sound, even if they have never seen the word before. This is how good readers learn new words.

When children read the words on the Decoding Power Pages, they should not be trying to find a 'match' with a word they know. All the words on Decoding Power Pages are regular—they can all be 'sounded out' without any guesswork. Some of the words are very unusual, like 'quern', 'bort' and 'loach'—but they are all real words.

Remember—you must always use the cursor. You must teach pupils to scan from left to right and to read every sound.

Do not give a tick for a 'good try'. Your pupil must get all the words on a line right, without any help, to earn a tick. If you think he will be able to get it right on his own, you can back up the cursor and let him try again, but do not let him struggle or guess. If he has forgotten the sounds or is unable to blend them, say the sounds yourself and let him say the word. If he is in a total muddle, model the whole process and then get him to repeat it. Always go back to any word you helped with—see **The Flashback Technique** on page 9.

DECODING ~ POWER ~ PAGE

If a pupil makes a mistake, back up the cursor and then sound out the word.

gut	egg	jet	cop	☑
sell	leg	hog	van	☑
mop	hen	nod	lip	☑
pit	off	bug	cab	☑
hot	till	job	men	☑
pin	set	can	tell	☑
did	mess	puff	kill	☑
has	yet	box	gun	☑
cut	bit	beg	cat	☑
dot	fog	sub	jazz	☑
lot	vat	hill	lass	☑
net	tax	ham	fit	☑

ee, ar, sh

Always use the cursor!

s<u>ee</u>	s<u>ee</u>m	<u>c</u><u>ar</u>	c<u>ar</u>t
wi<u>sh</u>	<u>sh</u>ip	bar	barn
Shep	park	meet	Carl
bark	dark	Josh	shut
Mark	keep	Bart	shed
weeds	yard	seen	Barb

Can Bart see in the dark?

Did Shep bark at the fat cop?

Josh shut his cart in the shed.

Will Carl meet Max in the park?

Can Mark keep his red car in the barn?

Has Barb seen the weeds in the yard?

12

DECODING ~ POWER ~ PAGE

Some of these words are unusual but they are all real words.

add	dud	jut	pug	☑
bee	shop	car	wish	☑
web	rudd	fuss	ebb	☑
ken	pun	wed	biff	☑
need	farm	meet	dark	☑
hiss	Ben	ell	kit	☑
rap	wig	boff	huss	☑
ship	keep	see	cash	☑
col	gig	mix	ted	☑
sat	jug	zap	met	☑
jam	pig	hut	tub	☑
six	tug	dad	zip	☑

13

er, th, ck

Do not award ticks for a 'good try'—your pupil will pay for it later!

this	with	her	Herb	✓
Jack	Jock	term	Beth	✓
bath	duck	maths	kerb	✓
Seth	Mack	teeth	Mick	✓
Vern	lock	pick	shock	✓
Merl	sick	muck	thick	✓

Herb got in the bath with his duck. ✓

Beth did well in maths this term. ✓

Tell Mick that his shark has sharp teeth. ✓

Mack and Seth will sit on the kerb. ✓

Will Jock and Vern pick the lock for you? ✓

Merl will feel sick if the muck is thick. ✓

DECODING POWER PAGE

Some of these words are unusual but they are all real words.

yon	mitt	bid	fen	☑
jerk	that	tick	duck	☑
week	rush	bark	sheep	☑
bib	fad	luff	Jess	☐
herd	than	with	nerd	☑
hard	posh	been	sham	☑
wen	moss	con	gob	☐
back	deck	thin	Serb	☐
part	mash	deep	far	☑
gas	kiss	hum	miss	☑
wax	hit	fat	hex	☑
dug	got	had	fin	☑

15

or, ch, qu

Always use the cursor!

Norm	chip	quiz	rich
quick	Seth	north	march
forth	cheek	quill	duck
quack	sick	thorn	porch
chop	beech	quit	such
quern	Chuck	torch	much

The Queen has had my fish and chips.

Why did that sheep get in the porch?

Did Rich get sick much in my car?

Chuck will kill you if that duck quacks.

Did Norm chop up that beech tree?

Seth will march north with you this week.

DECODING ⚡ POWER ⚡ PAGE

Do not award ticks for a 'good try'—your pupil will pay for it later!

quick	rich	sort	charm	☐
Dick	kerb	Thor	Perth	☐
bar	seen	rash	darn	☐
quid	porch	quiff	forth	☐
Jack	perm	teeth	thorp	☐
cuff	bod	hem	nub	☐
worn	chap	quin	nor	☐
tern	pith	lick	chuck	☐
feed	cart	shun	mark	☐
fern	moth	thick	pack	☐
quack	fork	quit	much	☐
jar	bash	lee	shin	☐

oy, ay, oa, oi, ai

Remember to practise the flashcards at least once a day!

boy	pay	coat	boil
pain	road	poach	Fay
foil	Roy	Gail	wait
coach	coin	joy	paid
join	boat	Joan	chain
Perth	quail	void	moan

Did Joan pay you much for that chain?

Who are the boys on the coach to Perth?

If Joy has paid, she can join us on my boat.

If you hit Roy hard, he will be in pain.

If we wait, Fay will poach six eggs for us.

Gail will need her coat if she waits for Joan.

DECODING POWER PAGE

If a pupil makes a mistake, back up the cursor and then sound out the word.

weep	shim	weed	darn	☐
boy	coat	day	rain	☑
goth	hers	shock	thill	☑
tort	quill	perch	chub	☐
road	join	toy	mail	☑
nosh	lard	beet	marsh	☑
berg	hack	perk	thorn	☑
goat	boil	pain	ray	☐
chick	quell	torch	ford	☑
lag	rid	wit	bob	☑
verb	thug	path	wack	☐
queen	North	chock	torn	☐

air, eer, oar, ore

Remember to practise the flashcards at least once a day!

b<u>eer</u>	m<u>ore</u>	Cl<u>air</u>	r<u>oar</u>
fair	soar	cheer	tore
air	queer	hoard	core
chair	board	wore	hair
peer	pair	boar	gore

Who will go to get more beer for the boys?

Clair wore a red coat to go to the fair.

If it is dark, you can see bats soar in the air.

Gail wore a pair of odd socks today.

Sit in that chair, if you feel a bit queer.

I tore my shorts on the nail in that board.

She will cheer up if I cut her hair.

DECODING ⚡ POWER ⚡ PAGE

> Do not award ticks for a 'good try'—your pupil will pay for it later!

vain	soap	coin	bay	☐
beer	more	fair	roar	☐
lark	jeep	harsh	shut	☐
foil	goal	may	Roy	☐
torn	chug	north	quill	☐
hair	wore	cheer	board	☐
sip	fad	lop	mug	☐
pert	mock	terse	chock	☐
fail	coach	pay	toil	☐
thug	quip	buck	verb	☐
sore	pair	jeer	hoard	☑
cord	beech	quack	march	☐

Mastery Test

Any pupil who does not pass this test must go back to page 11. This is very important—a child who is struggling will not be learning. Contrary to what you would think, most children do not mind going back. It's better than getting things wrong. **If your pupil is struggling consider using Dancing Bears A instead—it has more practice and introduces new material more slowly.**

If the pupil needs to go back, use a different coloured pencil for ticking the boxes.

Timed reading: 'Pass' mark is 15 seconds per line.

boy	torch	Beth	quit	☐
say	queen	fork	chop	☐
way	much	luck	north	☐

Reading accuracy: Pass mark is one mistake.
Do not prompt. You may allow the pupil to self correct, but you cannot say anything except "Try again".

I had to give my toys to Mark. ☐

If you are quick, you may feed the shark. ☐

Have you paid for the fish and chips? ☐

Roy had to go to the farm in the dark. ☐

Why did you pay so much for that lock? ☐

FAST TRACK

Advanced Flashcards:

The advanced flashcards are printed on blue card. They should be cut up and used in just the same way as the basic flashcards. Some of these cards represent two phonemes (eg, 'oke and ake'). Your pupil will already be familiar with words such as *give* and *horse*, that end in silent 'e', but this is the first introduction to the Split Digraph or Magic 'E' Rule. Model the sounds without breaking them down. There is no need to explain the rule unless your pupil is really confused by the silent 'e'.

Final Consonant Blends:

Most children will master consonant blends easily with the help of the following sheets.

You will notice that the words are arranged in pairs. The first is a CVC word and the second is the same word with another consonant added. The first pair is:

    ten   tent

By now your pupil will be able to read 'ten' easily. He should be able to add the final consonant without too much difficulty but if he cannot, you will have to do a bit of oral blending for him. For instance, say the word 'ten'—pause, then add the final /t/. Then ask him what the word was. Obviously, you do not give him a tick until he can do this entirely on his own.

DECODING ⚡ POWER ⚡ PAGE
Final Consonant Blends

ten	tent	bus	bust	☐
tan	tank	pin	pink	☐
pass	past	loss	lost	☐
hill	hilt	ran	rant	☐
sun	sunk	chum	chump	☐
gun	gunk	sill	silk	☐
shell	shelf	hem	hemp	☐
dam	damp	hell	held	☐
Bess	best	well	Welsh	☐
gull	gulf	pun	punch	☐
gas	gasp	bus	busk	☐
doll	dolt	ben	bend	☐

DECODING ~ POWER ~ PAGE

Some of these words are unusual but they are all real words.

chore	seer	chair	soar	☐
quern	thick	erse	thud	☐
bait	foam	Hoy	quail	☐
morn	queen	chard	gorse	☐
reel	marl	hash	sharp	☐
pore	jeer	hoard	air	☐
check	verb	lack	with	☐
tail	day	foal	soil	☐
cork	chart	quiz	lord	☐
heel	art	shall	park	☐
cos	god	nib	ten	☐
York	larch	quiz	porch	☐

FAST TRACK

Fluency Reading:

Timed readings will help your child read words quickly and automatically. At first, the times are very easy. Some children get nervous when they are being tested, and you do not want them to be worried by the stopwatch. For real timing-phobics, sit the child with his back to a wall clock with a second hand.

Frame the first word in the line with the cursor, and then say 'go'. Move the cursor as fast as the pupil can read. Record the time on the sheet and tick the line off if the pupil reads every word within 10 seconds. The usual rules apply—if the child makes a mistake, you can move the cursor back and let him have another go but you cannot give him any help. Model any word he gets stuck on and re-time that line the next day.

Unless the pupil is extremely slow, he will want to try for bonus points. You can award one bonus point if the pupil reads the line in 8 seconds, and two bonus points if he reads it in 6 seconds. You can motivate your pupil with stickers or rewards when he gets enough bonus points. If the pupil wants to have another go at a line to win a bonus point, he must wait until the following day.

Story:

The story is intended as an entertainment. There is no tick-box for this exercise but if the pupil struggles with a sentence he should be encouraged to read it again. It may be a good idea to read the story twice to improve fluency. Model any words the pupil gets stuck on.

FLUENCY READING

☐ Pass: 10 sec. ☆ Bonus: 8 sec. ★ Double Bonus: 6 sec.

gut	sell	mop	pit	☐ ☆ ★
hot	pin	did	has	☐ ☆ ★
cut	egg	leg	hen	☐ ☆ ★
off	till	set	mess	☐ ☆ ★
yet	bit	jet	hog	☐ ☆ ★
nod	bug	job	can	☐ ☆ ★
puff	box	beg	cop	☐ ☆ ★
van	lip	cab	men	☐ ☆ ★
tell	kill	gun	cat	☐ ☆ ★
dot	vat	ham	tax	☐ ☆ ★
net	hill	lot	fog	☐ ☆ ★

On the Way to the shop.

Mark was lost. His mum had sent him to get a loaf and some milk for lunch. He went up the road to the shop and then he met Vern. Vern was a big boy and he had a pet snail. "You must meet my snail." Vern said. "Froid is my pet snail. He has just had beer and roast beef for lunch. See him sit in his chair and rest."

Vern let Mark pick up Froid, who was Vern's pet snail. Vern let Mark pick up his chair. "Froid has wet feet." said Mark. Vern said, "Why, yes, Froid is a snail!"

Next, we will tell you why Mark got lost.

oi, air, eer, ore

Remember to practise the flashcards at least once a day!

joint	pair	more	deer
chair	queer	point	tore
moist	wore	cheer	hair
pore	lair	moist	leer

We need some more chairs here.

The coat she wore is moist with the rain.

Joy went to the shop for some more foil.

There are six deer in the park.

Where did you get that pair of red socks?

Point to the boy who tore his vest.

My nan wore her hair in a bun.

DECODING ~ POWER ~ PAGE

Do not award ticks for a 'good try'—your pupil will pay for it later!

kip	null	yam	bun	☐
mink	weld	risk	past	☐
hair	fore	peer	boar	☐
ant	sing	fond	daft	☐
joint	lore	fair	leer	☐
Joan	aim	roach	Fay	☐
barn	lush	sash	seek	☐
board	pair	moist	pore	☐
pong	imp	lunch	went	☐
nick	kerf	term	thug	☐
worn	quench	chill	port	☐
sung	punch	belt	end	☐

FLUENCY READING

☐ Pass: 10 sec. ☆ Bonus: 8 sec. ★ Double Bonus: 6 sec.

jam	six	gas	wax	☐ ☆ ★
jug	pig	tug	kiss	☐ ☆ ★
ham	zap	hut	dad	☐ ☆ ★
hum	fat	had	jazz	☐ ☆ ★
zip	miss	hex	fin	☐ ☆ ★
sub	lass	fit	jam	☐ ☆ ★
six	dug	got	hit	☐ ☆ ★
yon	jerk	week	bib	☐ ☆ ★
mitt	that	rush	fad	☐ ☆ ★
bid	tick	bark	luff	☐ ☆ ★
fen	duck	sheep	Jess	☐ ☆ ★

Off to the Dump.

Mark let Vern have his pet snail back. Froid the snail just sat in his chair and Vern let him rest. Vern said, "You must go to the dump with me. We can have lots of fun at the dump." Mark said, "But I must go to the shop and get a loaf and some milk for my lunch. Mum will be mad if I am not back". Vern said, "It will be quick if we fly. You can fly if you try!"

So Mark and Vern set off to fly to the dump. They got to the dump with Froid, the pet snail. The dump was big and it was full of junk. It had a pong of damp dog. "We can have lots of fun in that hill of moist muck!" said Vern.

Can you think why Mark got lost?

DECODING POWER PAGE

Remember to practise the flashcards at least once a day!

jail	soy	oat	quoit	☐
beer	more	fair	roar	☐
born	quilt	chip	for	☐
moist	wimp	hang	fact	☐
verve	teem	mush	hark	☐
shore	fair	board	deer	☐
chimp	bung	ramp	pink	☐
huff	bell	odd	lax	☐
think	erne	muck	chick	☐
serf	thank	pick	perch	☐
joint	kiln	dump	song	☐
cot	lap	rut	bus	☐

FLUENCY READING

☐ Pass: 10 sec.   ☆ Bonus: 8 sec.   ★ Double Bonus: 6 sec.

mat	map	mud	fox	☐ ☆ ★
pill	bud	bet	dux	☐ ☆ ★
kid	bed	sip	tap	☐ ☆ ★
tan	tip	ran	yell	☐ ☆ ★
fell	pan	tag	boss	☐ ☆ ★
herd	gas	back	dug	☐ ☆ ★

Bart, the Junk-Yard Dog.

So Mark, Vern and Froid went to the hill of moist muck. Froid was just a short snail, so he had to go. Then they met Bart, the junk-yard dog. Bart had the pong of a damp dog. But then Bart *was* a damp dog. Bart said, "Will you join me for some roast toad? I have a pair of hot toads in my hill of moist muck."

Vern said, "Froid can not have roast toad for he is a snail. Can we have a short shark?"
Bart said, "The last short shark went off to see the Queen. But you can have a sharp shark."
Mark said, "Thank you so much, but I must tell my mum or she will be mad."

Next, you will see why Mark did not get his lunch.

DECODING ⚡ POWER ⚡ PAGE

Some of these words are unusual but they are all real words.

sore	pair	jeer	soar	☑
yarn	gosh	feel	teen	☑
chop	bort	quill	pork	☑
zest	gasp	melt	chink	☑
bill	rip	bad	hug	☑
ore	lair	queer	roar	☑
win	gaff	Max	rig	☑
ring	quest	pelt	jilt	☑
load	coy	quail	void	☐
say	her	quit	coin	☐
bunch	elf	foist	bang	☐
frog	twin	still	snap	☐

FLUENCY   READING

☐ Pass: 10 sec.   ☆ Bonus: 8 sec.   ★ Double Bonus: 6 sec.

sum	get	dog	pub	☐ ☆ ★
bat	sad	hop	log	☐ ☆ ★
fad	than	posh	moss	☐ ☆ ★
fix	big	nut	pop	☐ ☆ ★
lit	mum	rug	let	☐ ☆ ★

Shark Oil.

Mark went with Vern, Froid and Bart to the deep pond, where they met Herb. Herb was the sharp shark. "I am glad you are here for lunch," he said. "My back is sore and I need some oil. Here is ten quid for some oil." Bart said, "There are lots of junk cars here. I can go and drain some oil, then we can boil a joint of beef. I will bark if I get lost."

Then Froid fell off his chair in to some moist muck. Vern said, "Can you see where Froid went?" Mark said, "Yes, he is in his shell. Shall I go and get my loaf and some milk?" But Bart was not back with the oil so they had to ask Herb to wait in the deep pond. It was dark in his shell so Froid went to sleep. "Who will tell my mum where I am?" Asked Mark.

Do you think Mark's mum was mad?

Mastery Test

Any pupil who does not pass this test must go back to page 24. This is very important—a child who is struggling will not be learning. Contrary to what you would think, most children do not mind going back. It's better than getting things wrong.

If the pupil needs to go back, use a different coloured pencil for ticking the boxes.

Timed reading: 'Pass' mark is 15 seconds per line.

more   bunch   coil   porch   ☐

fair   damp   moat   kerb   ☐

beer   melt   quail   point   ☐

Reading accuracy: Pass mark is one mistake.
Do not prompt. You may allow the pupil to self correct, but you cannot say anything except "Try again".

Did you see where the boat went? ☐

A thin, card box will not keep you dry if it rains hard. ☐

Who was the boy in the torn coat? ☐

You must board the coach to Perth here. ☐

There is no more of that beef joint left. ☐

DECODING ⚡ POWER ⚡ PAGE
Initial Consonant Blends

stop	play	flag	☑
drop	glad	swim	☑
grab	spell	slip	☑
brick	clay	trick	☑
skill	black	crab	☑
frog	swot	twin	☑
snap	dwell	smug	☑
skim	Gwen	twill	☑
cram	grin	plot	☑
snob	pram	fray	☑
drip	cliff	spun	☑
slam	grid	skull	☐

DECODING ~ POWER ~ PAGE

Do not award ticks for a 'good try'—your pupil will pay for it later!

oat	rail	hoist	bay	☑
hat	mid	yes	fed	☑
clock	flag	pram	swim	☑
quell	horn	char	cord	☑
blot	droll	flock	grit	☑
lung	chunk	act	vest	☑
buck	sock	them	her	☑
twill	slop	green	crab	☑
sheer	bore	fair	oar	☑
pail	quip	horse	joy	☑
prim	grab	drill	blob	☑
teeth	hush	chard	shark	☑

FLUENCY READING

☐ Pass: 10 sec. ☆ Bonus: 8 sec. ★ Double Bonus: 6 sec.

hid	dig	bad	bell
hug	box	rat	nap
fuzz	pin	bag	hip
with	been	con	thin
him	pot	cot	lap
rut	bus	not	lad

A Crock of Eels.

Mark and Vern left the deep pond to see where Bart had got to. Bart was a damp dog and damp dogs smell, so Mark and Vern just had to sniff. Herb the sharp shark had to stay in the deep pond for he did not have a bus pass. Froid was still stuck in the moist muck, yet he still did not have his chair.

"I can smell a strong pong," said Vern, "so Bart must be here." But Bart was not here and he was not there. Mark said, "Here is a crock of eels. They smell a lot. They must be the things we can smell." Vern said, "Ask that eel if he has seen Bart, the junk-yard dog." But the eel did not say where Bart was. He just swam in his crock and stank. Mark said, "I must get back or my mum will tell the cops that I am lost."

Do you think that Mark was lost?

Consonant Blends

Always use the cursor!

fleet	storm	sleep	start	train
float	creep	spoil	trail	dress
swim	Fred	bleed	play	clock

a + way = away
to + day = today

Put the toys away and go to sleep.

I think Joan snores in her sleep.

They will start off up the trail at six o'clock.

Come here and play with my black train.

Gail had some green snails for lunch.

You will spoil that dress if you paint in it.

Fred went away on the train today.

Gwen can swim with a float.

DECODING POWER PAGE

Some of these words are unusual but they are all real words.

skid	glut	fled	class	☑
tuck	perch	maths	neck	☑
fee	shot	feet	carp	☑
chat	ford	tore	quick	☑
clink	bluff	grass	plan	☑
bath	herb	kick	ruck	☑
moan	play	gait	coil	☑
lore	pair	oar	seer	☑
tuft	silk	ask	hump	☑
parch	fail	leech	hock	☑
crack	drip	glass	swig	☑
woad	joint	stay	laid	☑

FLUENCY READING

☐ Pass: 10 sec. ☆ Bonus: 8 sec. ★ Double Bonus: 6 sec.

kin	less	cup	bill	☐ ☆ ★
rip	dip	doll	hat	☐ ☆ ★
mid	yes	fed	gum	☐ ☆ ★
sham	gob	far	miss	☐ ☆ ★
add	bee	web	ken	☐ ☆ ★
need	hiss	rap	ship	☐ ☆ ★

Groyne, the Grey-Green Goat.

Who do you think Mark and Vern ran in to on the way to the hill of moist muck? They met Groyne, the grey-green goat, who wore his hair in a quiff. Vern said, "My pal Mark needs to get a loaf and some milk for his mum. Is there a store in this dump?"

Groyne bit a chunk of brick and had a munch

on some foil. Then he said, "You must ask Bart, the damp dog. I just have my lunch here."

Mark said, "We must go back to the deep pond and get Froid, the short snail. He must miss his chair." Groyne, the grey-green goat, said, "You must not trust Herb, the sharp shark, for he has no bus pass." So Vern paid Groyne six coins for his torch and they went back on the trail to the deep pond.

Where do you think Bart, the junk-yard dog, was?

DECODING ~ POWER ~ PAGE

If a pupil makes a mistake, back up the cursor and then sound out the word.

chuck	verse	kith	peck	☐
grip	flop	clam	skill	☐
torch	corm	cheep	quit	☐
tart	josh	yard	beef	☐
pang	mend	nest	film	☐
more	beer	Claire	hoard	☐
loach	hay	loin	Cain	☐
punch	soy	quilt	long	☐
fore	sing	aim	lush	☐
boar	daft	went	thug	☐
king	aft	bank	champ	☐
norm	chit	orfe	inch	☐

FLUENCY READING

☐ Pass: 10 sec.   ☆ Bonus: 8 sec.   ★ Double Bonus: 6 sec.

dud	shop	rudd	pun	☐ ☆ ★
farm	Ben	wig	rid	☐ ☆ ★
keep	gig	jut	car	☐ ☆ ★
fuss	wed	meet	ell	☐ ☆ ★
quid	jack	cuff	worn	☐ ☆ ★
boff	see	mix	pug	☐ ☆ ★
wish	ebb	biff	dark	☐ ☆ ★

Mark and the Shard.

Mark and Vern left Groyne, the grey-green goat, who wore his hair in a quiff, and went off on the trail to the deep pond. On the way, Mark slid on some slick clay. He fell on a shard of glass and cut his arm.

Vern said, "I will put some mud on the cut so it will not bleed. It is not a bad cut and I think you will live." Then they saw a damp dog come up the hill. "It must be Bart," said Mark, "I can tell by the smell."

Bart said, "I live in that smart shack on the steep hill. Come up the stairs with me and I will give you some lunch." But then Mark saw Froid, the short snail. He had green paint on his shell. He was still stuck in the moist muck.

Do you think Mark got his lunch?

Consonant Blends

Remember to practise the flashcards at least once a day!

scarf	shelf	sweet	point	☐
free	moist	snarl	twerp	☐
braid	blink	gloat	stoat	☐
smart	green	stay	think	☐

> rain + storm = rainstorm

The rainstorm has left the soil moist. ☐

I saw your green scarf by the chair. ☐

If you are smart, you will stay away today. ☐

Could you tell your stoat not to snarl? ☐

Could you point to the deer you saw? ☐

That twerp thinks the sweets are free. ☐

Faith wore her hair in a green braid. ☐

Could you put your torch on the shelf? ☐

DECODING ~ POWER ~ PAGE

Always use the cursor!

puck	berth	dock	then	☐
twig	fret	snip	plum	☐
Ark	meek	short	tosh	☐
elm	dung	mist	quench	☐
verse	sack	berth	luck	☐
peel	arm	shell	seed	☐
flap	drop	bran	stab	☐
sheer	core	fair	boar	☐
foil	goad	boy	ail	☐
shelf	rung	pond	mint	☐
quick	kerb	rash	fifth	☐
mort	chug	quench	morse	☐

FLUENCY READING

☐ Pass: 10 sec. ☆ Bonus: 8 sec. ★ Double Bonus: 6 sec.

kit	huss	cash	Ted	☑ ☆ ★
yon	jerk	week	bib	☑ ☆ ★
herd	hard	den	back	☑ ☆ ★
part	mitt	that	rush	☑ ☆ ★
fad	than	posh	moss	☑ ☆ ★
deck	mash	bid	tick	☑ ☆ ★
bark	luff	with	been	☑ ☆ ★
con	thin	deep	fen	☑ ☆ ★
duck	sheep	Jess	herd	☑ ☆ ★
buff	buck	fee	nag	☐ ☆ ★
bath	dish	tod	puck	☐ ☆ ★

Root Beer with Bart.

Bart had said that his shack was smart, for it had a coat of fresh paint, but it was big as well. They went up the stairs and at the top they saw Bart's maid. She had to mop up the muck, and in a dump this can be a hard job.

"You can put Froid's chair here by this pail of snails." said Bart. "Here is the root beer. If you wait, Meg, the maid, will bring you a glass. Then she will put lunch on the oak board by the stairs."

Mark said, "I am not a big boy and my mum says I must not drink much root beer. Can I have a glass of milk?" Vern said, "I am a big boy and I can drink lots of root beer. Put my glass here. Cheers!"

Do you still think that Mark got his lunch?

DECODING ⚡ POWER ⚡ PAGE

> Do not award ticks for a 'good try'—your pupil will pay for it later!

part	deep	posh	leek	☑
swill	glad	brim	drop	☑
peep	lard	shed	geese	☑
loft	junk	kelp	ink	☑
shack	perch	Seth	pick	☑
brass	grim	spot	swam	☑
pair	shore	deer	oar	☑
Jock	herd	them	lock	☑
tar	baize	felt	tee	☑
noise	sung	jail	wimp	☑
moist	Clem	frail	inch	☑
Jain	nark	pluck	skiff	☑

FLUENCY READING

☐ Pass: 10 sec. ☆ Bonus: 8 sec. ★ Double Bonus: 6 sec.

peel	mess	sock	shot	☐ ☆ ★
teg	seem	duff	berth	☐ ☆ ★
arm	them	feet	doff	☐ ☆ ★
kick	card	will	dock	☐ ☆ ★
shell	fib	her	carp	☐ ☆ ★
cox	ruck	lash	fid	☐ ☆ ★
then	seed	fern	quack	☐ ☆ ★
sham	gob	Herb	far	☐ ☆ ★
fern	quack	jar	lag	☐ ☆ ★
verb	queen	heel	cos	☐ ☆ ★
rid	thug	north	art	☐ ☆ ★

Mark has a bath.

Mark said, "Could I have a bath now? My hair is full of moist muck." Bart the damp dog said, "You can go up the stairs and have a bath. Be quick now, or you will miss your lunch." So Mark went up the stairs. The stairs went up and up. They went up so far that Mark could see the stars in the sky.

At last Mark got to the bath. He got in the hot tub with some soap and had a long soak. Then he had to wait for Meg the maid, who had some fresh socks. She said, "Here, let me give you this dress to put on now." "But I am not a lass," Mark said, "I am a boy!" But Mark had to put the dress on or he would have had to go to lunch in just his socks.

Mark got back but there was no lunch. Groyne, the grey-green goat, was there. The quiff in his hair was stiff with mud. "Have a munch on this board," he said. Vern, Bart and Froid had drunk so much root beer they could not

stand up. "Give a glass of root beer to Herb," said Bart, "He cannot come up the stairs, for he is a sharp shark." Mark had to ask, "How did Herb get here? Has he paid ten quid for a bus pass?"

Do you think Mark will ever get his mum some milk and a loaf?

Do you think Mark will ever get some lunch?

Mastery Test

Any pupil who does not pass this test must go back to page 40. This is very important—a child who is struggling will not be learning. Contrary to what you would think, most children do not mind going back. It's better than getting things wrong.

If the pupil needs to go back, use a different coloured pencil for ticking the boxes.

Timed reading: 'Pass' mark is 15 seconds per line.

spark	score	creep	tray	☐
stern	point	float	quack	☐
brain	chair	coy	stork	☐

Reading accuracy: Pass mark is one mistake.
Do not prompt. You may allow the pupil to self correct, but you cannot say anything except "Try again".

There is still some corn left in the grain store. ☐

Could you put your coat next to her cloak? ☐

Last week, Joan wore her hair in a braid. ☐

We saw where Roy hid his sports bag. ☐

Clair will paint the boards with a green stain. ☐

Affixes.

This is the first Decoding Sheet with words which are not pronounced as they are written. With most words that end in *-ed*, you do not pronounce the 'e'. The word *spelled* is pronounced *speld* or *spelt*.

When you add *-ed* to words that end in 'd' or 't', you **do** voice the 'e', but it is an unstressed *schwa* sound. In other words *needed* is pronounced *need'd*.

In later sheets, some words have a root which is not used on its own, for example: *disturb*. This is indicated by printing *turb* in italics.

Remember, if your pupil cannot read the word straight away, you **must** model it and get him to repeat it. Then go back to the word a few seconds later. *Never—ever—encourage a pupil to guess.*

-ing, -er, -all, -ly, -ed

If a pupil makes a mistake, back up the cursor and then sound out the word.

sleep	sleeping	tall	taller	☐
quick	quickly	rest	rested	☐
go	going	short	shorter	☐
hard	hardly	ask	asked	☐
cry	crying	small	smaller	☐

Mark said that we must get going quickly. ☐

Now you have had a sleep, do you feel rested? ☐

Vern asked for a smaller bag of chips. ☐

The taller boy was hardly crying at all. ☐

Bart needs a shorter sleeping bag. ☐

fish	fishing	hard	harder	☐
rain	raining	start	started	☐
miss	missed	hang	hanging	☐
part	partly	munch	munched	☐

It has just started raining a lot harder. ☐

Do you think we should go fishing or flying? ☐

Ray missed the coat hanging on the back wall. ☐

Max munched on his pork chop all day. ☐

DECODING ~ POWER ~ PAGE

Always use the cursor!

spot	plum	drab	grill	☐
tall	running	fitted	cutter	☐
bunk	end	fang	jolt	☐
hotly	wishing	fatter	helped	☐
coarse	steer	flair	score	☐
matted	quickly	fall	nipper	☐
stay	float	snail	spoil	☐
runner	hall	hitting	lastly	☐
breech	quest	horn	scorch	☐
landed	taller	flatly	calling	☐
erst	filth	snack	forth	☐
handed	partly	small	running	☐
sleet	crash	scar	keel	☐
ball	pinned	asking	zipper	☐

Cloze Sentences:

Pupils enjoy these exercises, and they get to practise using the words they have learnt by reading them in meaningful sentences.

In the box at the top of each page, you will find the new words that the pupil will need in order to read the sentences. Move the cursor smoothly and quickly across the letters reveal the entire word. If the pupil cannot read the word, model the correct response. Using the Flashback Technique (see page 9), repeat each word until firm.

Reading the sentences:

For this exercise you will need a blank sheet of thin card about A6 in size. Cover the sentence and ask the pupil to read the three 'answer' words underneath the sentence first, using the cursor as usual. (This is to prevent him guessing at the missing word.) Then let the pupil read the sentence, still using the cursor. If the pupil reads the sentence and selects the right answer without prompting, circle the correct word. (The pupil **should not** write the word—this takes too long and is a distraction.) Otherwise, the sentence should be repeated in a subsequent lesson. If the pupil does not know the meaning of a word, explain it as simply as possible—but in no circumstances encourage pupils to guess at words they have read incorrectly.

> should, would, could, how, now, your

Joan left her desk just now to get her ___.

        coal   coat   coast

How did your car get a dent in the ___?

        bath   back   bunk

Your dog should not be left in the ___.

        lung   pong   car

We must get going ___ or we could miss the train.

        quickly   hardly   partly

FLUENCY READING

☐ Pass: 10 sec.   ☆ Bonus: 8 sec.   ☆☆ Double Bonus: 6 sec.

god	larch	thick	quit	☐ ☆ ☆
nib	quiz	pack	much	☐ ☆ ☆
park	ten	porch	quick	☐ ☆ ☆
cuff	worn	tern	feed	☐ ☆ ☆
rich	kerb	seen	torch	☐ ☆ ☆
quiff	teeth	hem	quint	☐ ☆ ☆

Groan, the Croaking Toad.

Vern, Bart and Froid rested by the stairs in Bart's shack. They had drunk all the beer. Groyne, the grey-green goat, who wore his hair in a quiff, munched on some foil by the oak board. Mark still wore a dress. Vern asked, "Where is my pal Mark? Have you seen a boy who is six?" Mark said, "I am Mark and I need some lunch." Bart, the damp dog said, "You could not be Mark, for he is a boy. You are in a dress, so you must be a girl."

So Mark had to get a shirt and some shorts so his pals would think that he was a boy. He left Bart's shack to see if he could find a store for shorts and shirts. He left Herb, the sharp shark, who was sleeping on his back with his bus pass stuck in his fin. He went past the hill of moist muck quickly and then he saw Groan, the croaking toad.

"Where are you going so fast, my girl, and why are you crying?" croaked Groan. Mark said, "I am crying for I need some lunch and I must find a shirt and a pair of shorts." Groan said, "Well, I sell all sorts of shorts and shirts. Come into my store now and you will find shirts and shorts for taller boys and smaller girls. We have

red shirts and green shorts. We have sharp shirts for shorter chaps, and we sell swell shorts for tall tramps. This is the best store in this dump."

Do you think Mark will find a shirt that will fit?

Do you think he has some cash to pay for a pair of shorts?

-es, -est, -ful, -less, -en, -y

If a pupil makes a mistake, back up the cursor and then sound out the word.

glass	glasses	strong	strongest	☐
fall	fallen	smell	smelly	☐
box	boxes	rot	rotten	☐
stick	sticky	small	smallest	☐
get	getting	rust	rusty	☐

You must pack the glasses in the strongest boxes. ☐

The fallen trees blocked the road. ☐

The smallest car is getting a bit rusty. ☐

The rotten pork was sticky and smelly ☐

tall	tallest	horse	horses	☐
feel	feeling	play	playful	☐
greed	greedy	luck	lucky	☐
thank	thankful	cord	cordless	☐
help	helpful	block	blocked	☐

The tallest horses are feeling playful. ☐

My dad is helpful with his cordless drill. ☐

You should be thankful that you are so lucky. ☐

Do not be so greedy or they will not feed you. ☐

DECODING POWER PAGE

Do not award ticks for a 'good try'—your pupil will pay for it later!.

costly	tapped	landing	harder	☐
rotten	tallest	foxes	happy	☐
hoarse	flair	adore	sneer	☐
handful	harmless	fatten	dotty	☐
stoat	hoist	quaint	stern	☐
horses	playful	smallest	spotless	☐
helper	rubbed	badly	falling	☐
brash	steep	float	scar	☐
sunken	hottest	musty	glasses	☐
score	queer	hair	oar	☐
gleeful	sharpen	feckless	sticky	☐
quitting	boxer	sorted	deftly	☐
clash	creel	broth	slain	☐
bosses	fattest	helpful	thicken	☐

very, many, any, one, none, done

Has anyone rung the bell for ___?

      lunch   lump   lamp

There are not very many trucks on this ___.

      roach   road   roast

They will clamp any cars that park in that ___.

      your   yard   yarn

None of my ___ are very smelly.

      songs   sharks   socks

FLUENCY READING

☐ Pass: 10 sec.　☆ Bonus: 8 sec.　☆☆ Double Bonus: 6 sec.

lick	shun	charm	Perth	☐ ☆ ☆
shim	coat	hers	quill	☐ ☆ ☆
join	lard	hack	boil	☐ ☆ ☆
horse	rack	paid	arch	☐ ☆ ☆
pail	parch	verse	oath	☐ ☆ ☆
form	eel	void	orb	☐ ☆ ☆

Hank, the Hunch-Backed Horse.

Mark missed Vern and his pet snail, Froid. He had to get some shorts and a shirt from Groan's store, or they would still think that he was a girl. He went deep into the store, where he saw more stacks of shorts and many hanging shirts. He saw backless dresses for girls, and boxes of the smallest coats for kids. Groan croaked, "Here are some smashing shirts for fishing, and some keen shorts for marching. Pick any one and try it on. But do not drop it in the muck, or you will spoil it."

Mark put on some green shorts for flying, and a red shirt that was not very long. "How much must I pay for this?" he asked. Groan croaked, "For you, my pal, that will be ten quid if you can pay now." Mark said, "But I just have six quid, and I still must get a loaf and some milk for my mum." Groan croaked, "That is very sad, but I cannot sell one shirt at a loss. You must go and get some more cash."

So Mark left Groan's store to go and get some more cash. He could not ask his pals for any coins, for they would just think that he was a small girl begging for cash, and they would give him none. Mark marched onto the moist muck, and then he met Hank, the hunch-backed horse. "Who are you? Where did you come from? Why are you crying? How did

you get here?" Hank asked. "I am Mark and I need some cash to get a pair of shorts and a shirt, so that my pals will think I am a boy." Mark said. "Why do you wish that your pals should think you are a boy? I can see that you are a girl. You should not try to trick your pals." said Hank. Mark just started crying harder.

Do you think Hank will help Mark get some more cash?

Do you think it would help if Mark had some lunch?

-ke Endings:

You pupil will already be familiar with words such as *give* and *horse* where the final 'e' is silent. The next page is the first introduction to the Split Digraph or Magic 'e' Rule. Do not start this sheet if your pupil has not mastered the advanced flashcards numbered 4 – 8. Make sure you reveal both parts of the digraph together with the cursor.

Some pupils have trouble getting used to these words and forget that the final 'e' makes the preceding vowel long.

If your pupil is struggling you can do one of two things: You can reverse the cursor so the pupil just sees the same ending as on the relevant flashcard—e.g. 'ake'. If he says it correctly, then take away the cursor and ask him "what word?"

Alternatively, you can take him through the Split Digraph Rule.

The Split Digraph Rule:

Point to the final 'e' and ask "What letter does this word end with?" Then point to the vowel and say "What is the *name* of this letter?" Then tell him "In this word, the 'e' makes the vowel say its own name.

You may have to say the sounds yourself (as in oral blending) and then ask the pupil to say the word.

If you pupil is confused by long 'u' words where the vowel is pronouced like the 'oo' in *moon*, model the word and ask him to repeat it. Use the Flashback Technique to reinforce the correction.

-ake, -eke, -ike, -oke, -uke

Remember to practise the flashcards at least once a day!

bake	cake	pike	strike	snake	☐
fake	brakes	bike	take	like	☐
quake	hike	shake	rake	Mike	☐

Did Gail bake a fresh cake? ☐

Do you think a pike will strike at my bait? ☐

Is that stuffed snake a fake? ☐

I would like to take you on a hike to the farm. ☐

A quake can shake things up a bit. ☐

My brakes stop my bike very quickly. ☐

take	trike	drake	like	lake	☐
Mike	wake	spike	sake	Jake	☐
flake	bike	stake	make	pike	☐

Mike hit the brass spike into the wall. ☐

For my sake, you should not wake me so quickly. ☐

Can Jake make a stake from this chunk of oak? ☐

If you hit a flint with steel, it will chip off a flake. ☐

Can I take my trike to the shop? ☐

Drakes and ducks like to swim on this lake. ☐

DECODING POWER PAGE

Always use the cursor!

helpless	fallen	smelly	wishes	☐
like	truck	duke	fake	☐
gall	telling	flatter	mended	☐
back	hike	puke	woke	☐
board	queer	snore	stair	☐
yuck	stoke	lake	bike	☐
playful	happen	luckless	thinnest	☐
brim	skip	twit	flip	☐
Peke	Jack	spoke	brick	☐
hardly	stall	quacking	bloater	☐
hake	nick	moke	luck	☐
mucky	wilful	bitten	backless	☐
faint	spoilt	sport	twerp	☐
loke	Jake	pick	spike	☐

> very, many, any, one, none, done

Did anyone see where she put her ___?

    drink   drop   drag

One of the sailing boats sank in the ___.

    pink   past   pond

How many glasses are on the top ___?

    shell   shelf   smack

Joy still has not paid the ___.

    barn   boat   bill

FLUENCY READING

☐ Pass: 10 sec. ☆ Bonus: 8 sec. ☆ Double Bonus: 6 sec.

nerve	boat	norm	lath	☐ ☆ ☆
loin	quiff	mesh	toad	☐ ☆ ☆
coy	fort	thick	vain	☐ ☆ ☆
beer	lark	foil	hair	☐ ☆ ☆
soap	more	jeep	goal	☐ ☆ ☆
wore	mock	coach	pair	☐ ☆ ☆

Jake, the Fake Snake.

Hank, the hunch-backed horse saw that Mark was crying and he felt bad. How could he help Mark? Mark needed someone to help him find some more cash so he could get a pair of shorts and a shirt from Groan's store. He needed to find ten quid to pay Groan, the croaking toad. Hank said, "I wish I could help you, but horses do not have any cash. But I can take you to see Jake, the fake snake, who is very helpful. You will like Jake."

Mark said, "I would like that very much. I would like to be a boy again. If I cannot get some cash from someone, I am done." So Hank and Mark went off to see Jake, the fake snake. "Jake lives at the far end of the tip." Hank said. "If anyone can tell you how to get some coins to pay for a shirt and a pair of shorts, it is Jake."

On the way from the hill of moist muck they had to take a path that went by a lake. They saw many ducks and drakes on the lake. They saw a drake flying back to Bart's shack and Mark wished he was with Vern and Froid, the pet snail. "I wish I had a bike," he said. "You would just get stuck in the muck if you had a bike," said Hank, the hunch-backed horse.

At last they got to the marsh where Jake, the fake snake lived. "Why do they call Jake a fake snake?" asked Mark.

Do you think Jake is a fake?

-ake, -eke, -ike, -oke, -uke

If a pupil makes a mistake, back up the cursor and then sound out the word.

stroke	likes	smoke	coke	Luke	☐
broke	duke	spoke	Jake	poke	☐
Mike	wake	bike	joke	bloke	☐

You may tell a joke if it is very funny. ☐

Take this coke to Jake, he is sitting by the lake. ☐

That bloke likes to have a smoke with his beer. ☐

The Duke spoke to Luke just now. ☐

Jake will wake up if you poke him in the ribs. ☐

I think Mike broke his bike chain. ☐

Luke	woke	spike	stoke	choke	☐
smoke	like	coke	pike	take	☐
bloke	nuke	lake	rake	fluke	☐

Luke woke up at six o'clock. ☐

Spike went on a trip to Stoke-on-Trent last week. ☐

It was just a fluke that the smoke woke Mike. ☐

You should take the rake and a digging fork. ☐

As I am broke, would you pay for my glass of coke? ☐

She would like to fish for pike in the lake. ☐

DECODING POWER PAGE

Some of these words are unusual but they are all real words.

fastest	sticky	torches	bashful	☐
hick	fluke	snake	pike	☐
needed	fairly	call	parting	☐
neck	track	stake	yoke	☐
store	cheer	hoard	bairn	☐
kick	make	Luke	stuck	☐
sweeten	chinless	thickest	tricky	☐
band	lend	runt	link	☐
poke	bake	chick	quake	☐
sweeper	railed	softly	ball	☐
muck	brick	slick	eke	☐
classes	wishful	chicken	helpless	☐
twain	gloat	joist	green	☐
quack	nuke	bloke	Dick	☐

> want, watch, walk, water, wash, above, love

The train struck a tree trunk that fell on the ___.

    take   track   tail

Jake loves to go ___ in the hills.

    watching   walking   wanting

Spike acted swiftly to stop the boy from jumping in the ___.

    want   water   walk

I would love to fly above the ___.

    water   watch   wash

FLUENCY READING

☐ Pass: 10 sec.　☆ Bonus: 8 sec.　☆☆ Double Bonus: 6 sec.

nerve	boat	norm	lath	☐ ☆ ☆
loin	quiff	mesh	toad	☐ ☆ ☆
coy	fort	thick	vain	☐ ☆ ☆
beer	lark	foil	hair	☐ ☆ ☆
soap	more	jeep	goal	☐ ☆ ☆
wore	mock	coach	pair	☐ ☆ ☆

Mastery Test

Any pupil who does not pass this test must go back to page 62. This is very important—a child who is struggling will not be learning. Contrary to what you would think, most children do not mind going back. It's better than getting things wrong.

If the pupil needs to go back, use a different coloured pencil for ticking the boxes.

Timed reading: 'Pass' mark is 15 seconds per line.

spotless	fair	sweeper	spoke	☐
sharpen	wake	boiled	twerp	☐
sailing	hoard	rusty	pike	☐
fluke	gloat	queer	boxes	☐

Reading accuracy: Pass mark is one mistake.
Do not prompt. You may allow the pupil to self correct, but you cannot say anything except "Try again".

Did Jake take his bike to go shopping? ☐

Mike drank his last coke quickly. ☐

Luke will not like all that smelly smoke very much. ☐

Spike needed the cordless drill to get one of his jobs done. ☐

At the Creepy Marsh.

Jake, the fake snake, lived in the creepy marsh at the far end of the tip. He stayed in a rusty car that had been left to rot in the dump. "How do you do," said Jake, who was very well-bred. "Take a chair and take a load off your feet. Would you like a drink?" Mark sat on a dusty chair, but it sank into the muck very quickly. "Could I have a glass of milk?" he asked. Jake said, "This is not your lucky day, for I have not got any milk. Would you like a beer?"

Hank, the hunch-backed horse, asked, "Do you make your beer with oats? Horses like oats and oats makes the strongest beer." So Jake, the fake snake, got some oat beer from a rusty car, but Mark could not drink much of it, for it was very strong. He asked, "Why do they call you a fake snake? You do not seem like a fake to me." Jake said, "You see I have ten feet and six hands. Snakes do not have hands and feet."

Then Hank, the hunch-backed horse, said, "My pal, Mark, needs your help. He needs to get some cash so that he can get a pair of shorts and a shirt from Groan, the croaking toad. How can he get some cash?" Jake, the fake snake hissed sharply. "It is very hard to find cash in this dump," he said. "I have none myself. You could go and see Mike, the greedy

loan shark. He lives next to Luke, the Duke of the tip. If you set off from here now, you can get there by dark."

Do you think Mark drank much oat beer?

Do you think Hank can stand up?

re-, be-, un-, ex-, pre-, dis-

If a pupil makes a mistake, back up the cursor and then sound out the word.

less	unless	port	report	☐
plain	explain	load	unload	☐
float	refloat	fore	before	☐
dress	undress	*rupt*	disrupt	☐

Luke will not let us go unless we unload the car. ☐

Could you explain why you got such a bad report? ☐

The divers had to refloat the sunken ship. ☐

At night we must undress before we go to bed. ☐

If you make a noise, you will disrupt Luke's sleep. ☐

tend	pretend	tract	distract	☐
cuss	discuss	mark	remark	☐
pay	repay	vent	prevent	☐
gust	disgust	well	unwell	☐

Did you discuss that smart remark with Joan? ☐

Do not distract Mike if he is trying to fix the car. ☐

Spike has to repay that loan before the week-end. ☐

Will the smell of rotten fish disgust Jake? ☐

If you do not want to go, pretend to be unwell. ☐

DECODING POWER PAGE

Do not award ticks for a 'good try'—your pupil will pay for it later!

clack	broke	drake	Mike	☐
replay	before	unpick	expel	☐
sharpest	soapy	boxes	thankful	☐
predict	disdain	refund	between	☐
wall	hoarding	fairer	joined	☐
unseen	explore	prevail	distress	☐
wake	suck	juke	choke	☐
aboard	flair	shore	jeer	☐
resent	beset	unfit	express	☐
batten	aimless	daftest	rainy	☐
pretend	dismiss	reject	before	☐
hack	joke	pluck	shake	☐
joint	frail	coast	steep	☐
unjust	explain	prevent	distort	☐

> want, watch, walk, water, wash, above, love

Beth was just saying how much she wanted to go ___.

    shopping   shipping   slipping

I keep hitting my hand with the ___.

    hamper   hammer   handed

I think you should ___ the dog.

    weld   walk   water

Could you bang in the nail with the ___?

    hanger   hopper   hammer

FLUENCY READING

☐ Pass: 10 sec. ☆ Bonus: 8 sec. ☆☆ Double Bonus: 6 sec.

beech	coin	fair	harsh	☐ ☆ ☆
jeer	quack	bay	roar	☐ ☆ ☆
toil	board	march	chore	☐ ☆ ☆
chard	hash	hoard	lack	☐ ☆ ☆
foal	quiz	soar	thug	☐ ☆ ☆
quail	gorse	sharp	air	☐ ☆ ☆

Hank Feels Unwell.

Hank, the hunch-backed horse, said, "I was so greedy that I drank more oat beer than I should have, and now I feel unwell. I want some water for a wash." Jake, the fake snake, said, "If you can walk to my bath, you can wash your hands and feet in hot water." "But horses do not have hands and feet," said Hank. Then he fell asleep with a crash.

Mark wanted to start walking up the road to find Mike, the loan shark, for he needed some cash to pay for a pair shorts and a shirt. He was fed up with his dress and he wanted to be a boy again. He wanted to see his pals, Vern and Froid. He wanted to see Bart, the junk-yard dog, too. He missed the smell of damp dog. So Mark said, "Who can take me to see Mike, the loan shark? I do not know the way and I do not want to get lost."

Jake the fake snake, said, "I would love to help you but I need ten socks and ten trainers, for I have ten feet. I am missing one of my trainers. But I will toss a pail of water on Hank and then he will wake up." Hank had to shake the water from his hair. He got up and said, "Why, we must march on. We must not slip on the slushy trail that takes us to see Mike, the loan shark. I will not let my pal fail." So they left Jake, the fake snake, who lived in a rusty car by the creepy marsh. They walked up the slushy trail that went by the reedy lake. "Unless we are quick, it will get dark before we find Mike, the loan shark," said Hank. Then he slipped on some sloppy muck and fell into a yucky pond.

Do you think that Hank will be a smelly horse?

89

-igh, -tch, -dge

Remember to practise the flashcards at least once a day!

hitch	lodge	fridge	night	edge	☐
ditch	light	switch	dredge	sludge	☐
catch	bridge	high	pitch	smudge	☐
bright	match	badge	notch	might	☐

Could Mike hitch a lift to the lodge? ☐

I like to raid the fridge at night. ☐

Do not stand on the edge of the ditch. ☐

You must switch off the lights at night. ☐

Did they dredge the sludge from the lake? ☐

right	judge	twitch	fetch	thigh	☐
stretch	scotch	midge	blight	clutch	☐
patch	slight	budge	sketch	fight	☐
fudge	itch	fright	dodge	sigh	☐

My dad asked me to fetch his glass of scotch. ☐

I have a slight twitch in my thigh. ☐

You will get a red blotch where the midge bit you. ☐

The judge said we should go right at the lights. ☐

Who trimmed that stretch of hedge? ☐

DECODING POWER PAGE

Always use the cursor!

refrain	begin	unstuck	exact	☐
catch	hedge	night	ditch	☐
quick	rake	smoke	eke	☐
judge	high	fetch	badge	☐
marches	needful	often	thankless	☐
etch	lodge	right	hatch	☐
prevent	display	reset	betray	☐
coyly	all	failing	thinner	☐
fridge	light	pitch	nudge	☐
flake	Luke	puck	shack	☐
tight	batch	ridge	fight	☐
unwell	expand	prefix	disrupt	☐
Ray	point	croak	fleet	☐
itch	fudge	sight	thatch	☐

Word building:

Most pupils like these exercises because they discover that reading long words is not really all that difficult once you know the building blocks or morphemes.

Most of the examples start off with a real word but there are some that start with a part of a word such as *cept* or *struct*. These are always in italics.

The only difficult items are the ones where the syllable structure changes in the middle of the line, these are marked with a star in the exercises. For instance:

        late   relate   *relative   relatively

Note that 'relate' breaks up as *re-late,* whereas 'relative' works out as *rel-uh-tive*. With words like this, you will probably have to tell your pupil the correct response the first time round. Do not forget to use the Flashback Technique.

With the cursor, segment the root word into phonemes as usual. Then with each successive word use the cursor to reveal each morpheme as a whole.

Wordbuilder

If a pupil makes a mistake, back up the cursor and then sound out the word.

load   reload   reloaded   ☐

tend   pretend   pretending   ☐

gust   disgust   disgusting   ☐

long   belong   belonging   belongings   ☐

The hunter reloaded his gun.   ☐

Jake was just pretending that he was broke.   ☐

Mike's dog smells very disgusting tonight.   ☐

You must take all of your belongings with you.   ☐

dress   undress   undressing   ☐

part   depart   departed   ☐

bid   forbid   forbidden   ☐

press   express   expressly   ☐

tract   distract distracted   ☐

I was undressing so that I could have a wash.   ☐

The driver was distracted and the car ran into a ditch. ☐

Playing football on the green is expressly forbidden.   ☐

The train to Leeds has just departed.   ☐

> want, watch, walk, water, wash, above, love

I put your hammer on the shelf above the ___.

    clod   clock   clog

You can sharpen a stick for toasting a ___.

    boy   bun   bunk

He kicked the ball above the goal ___.

    keener   keeper   killer

I want to watch him wash the black ___.

    duck   dog   drink

FLUENCY READING

☐ Pass: 10 sec.　☆ Bonus: 8 sec.　★ Double Bonus: 6 sec.

leer	held	toil	lamp	☐ ☆ ★
cheep	dunk	verve	tank	☐ ☆ ★
deed	chair	jump	loath	☐ ☆ ★
mink	hair	ant	Joan	☐ ☆ ★
aim	lush	imp	kerf	☐ ☆ ★
quench	yam	risk	peer	☐ ☆ ★

Mike, the Loan Shark.

Mark watched Hank, the hunch-backed horse drag himself from the sludge in the yucky pond. Hank was reeking of rotten eggs and sticky weeds were hanging from his neck. Hank kept slipping back as he walked up the bank back to the slushy trail. Mark said, "You are a right sight and you are such a smelly horse." Hank said, "I am just a horse and all horses are slightly smelly. We must walk quickly if we want to find Mike, the loan shark before dark."

On the way, Hank pointed to all of the best sights in the tip. There were junk fridges sunk into patches of green sludge. They saw stacks of rotten spuds and lots of stinking fish. Hank said, "I like this dump. It is the best junk-yard in the land."

Mike, the loan shark lived in a very smart lake with his pal, Patch, the pointless pike. Mike was very rich and he liked to play with his posh train set. His train could take him to Groan's store or it could take him to the pub for a drink. Mike was very flash and he wore lots of bling. He had five studs and a gold chain in his fin. "How can I help you?" he asked. Mark said, "I need some cash so I can get a shirt and a pair shorts. I am not a girl so I should not have to dress in a frock. If you can loan me six quid, all will be well."

Mike waited a bit, and then he asked, "How can you repay

me? You are just a small girl. Do you have a job?" Mark said, "I have a job just finding lunch in this dump. But if you loan me six quid, my mum will repay you." Mike said, "I cannot loan you any cash unless you have a job. If you need a job, you should go to see Luke, the Duke of the tip. He can help you get a job." Then Mike, the loan shark, swam off with his pal, Patch, the pointless pike.

Do you think Hank will have a wash?

ir, ur, -ce, -ge

Always use the cursor!

large	lice	charge	cage	bird	☐
Bruce	choice	girl	hurry	church	☐
shirt	price	pence	urge	dance	☐

Some very large lice are sleeping in my bed. ☐

What did they charge you for that bird cage? ☐

I think that Bruce made the right choice. ☐

The girls should hurry up if they are going to church. ☐

You can have that shirt for the price of ten pence! ☐

Joyce	voice	strange	stage	right	☐
twice	change	birch	fence	hurt	☐
Grace	burn	since	Greece	turn	☐
page	face	dirt	nice	birth	☐

Do you think that Joyce has a strange voice? ☐

If you turn right, you will fall off the stage. ☐

We had to change trains twice on the way to Leeds. ☐

Can you see that small bird up in the birch tree? ☐

Grace hurt her leg jumping the fence. ☐

My sunburn hurts since we got back from Greece. ☐

DECODING POWER PAGE

Do not award ticks for a 'good try'—your pupil will pay for it later!

hutch	edge	sigh	twitch	☐
large	girl	nice	burn	☐
resit	beyond	unhappy	extend	☐
mice	cage	turn	bird	☐
take	coke	chuck	bike	☐
firm	pence	fringe	curl	☐
bridge	bright	stitch	budge	☐
richest	lucky	blushes	painful	☐
burst	skirt	place	barge	☐
prepaid	disarm	reload	belay	☐
huge	curve	prince	fir	☐
might	latch	grudge	thigh	☐
hoarded	jointed	queerly	falling	☐
ledge	fright	scotch	sludge	☐

Wordbuilder

Remember to practise the flashcards at least once a day!

dress	address	addressed	☐
plain	explain	explained	☐
just	adjust	adjusting	☐
want	wanted	unwanted	☐

Is that letter addressed to me? ☐

Bruce just explained how to make a bridge. ☐

Grace is adjusting the chain on her bike. ☐

You could give your unwanted shirts to Royce. ☐

port	report	reported	☐
act	exact	exactly	☐
mit	admit	admitted	☐
play	replay	replaying	☐
pect	expect	expecting	☐

Joyce has reported her cat missing. ☐

Luke admitted that he broke the glass. ☐

Martha is expecting you back for lunch. ☐

I am fed up with replaying that film. ☐

Your report will be bad if your sums are not exactly right. ☐

> cook, book, look, foot, good, took, what, when, which

My gran is a very good ___.

        coal   cook   coat

Madge took a good look at the ___.

        bright   book   budge

When did Joyce cook that ___ cake?

        foot   thatch   fudge

Which foot did you ___?

        hurt   hurl   hurst

FLUENCY READING

☐ Pass: 10 sec. ☆ Bonus: 8 sec. ☆☆ Double Bonus: 6 sec.

fond	roach	sash	lunch	☐ ☆ ☆
boar	daft	Fay	seek	☐ ☆ ☆
oat	chip	hang	mush	☐ ☆ ☆
hark	deer	pink	lax	☐ ☆ ☆
moist	carve	shore	chimp	☐ ☆ ☆
quilt	wimp	teem	fair	☐ ☆ ☆

Mastery Test

Any pupil who does not pass this test must go back to page 83. This is very important—a child who is struggling will not be learning. Contrary to what you would think, most children do not mind going back. It's better than getting things wrong.

If the pupil needs to go back, use a different coloured pencil for ticking the boxes.

Timed reading: 'Pass' mark is 15 seconds per line.

pitch	remark	rake	hardly	☐
biggest	fight	unless	choke	☐
nuke	joist	bridge	pretend	☐
discuss	trike	chore	match	☐

Reading accuracy: Pass mark is one mistake.

Do not prompt. You may allow the pupil to self correct, but you cannot say anything except "Try again".

You must not disturb Luke before lunch. ☐

Spike got a red blotch where the midge bit him. ☐

The farmer dug a ditch to prevent the water from getting in. ☐

Could you explain why you forgot to switch off the lights? ☐

Luke, the Duke of the Dump.

Mike, the loan shark, swam back and said to Mark, "You seem like a nice kid. You can take my train to see Luke, the Duke of the dump. Take your pal, Hank, with you and you can catch the six o'clock train." Mark thanked Mike. He walked ten paces up the road with Hank, then they turned right to get to the railway. They boarded the train and sat in some soft chairs, for they were going first-class.

A large man with a badge asked them, "Can I see your passes?" Hank said, "Mike, the loan shark, said we could catch a lift on his train. You would not want to mess with Mike. We are going to see Luke, the Duke of the dump." The large man with the badge scratched his shirt, which was full of mice. He said, "Then it must be alright. If Mike is your pal, there will be no charge for this trip. Have a nice day, and do not forget to change trains at the church by the strange bridge."

Hank said to Mark, "This is just grand. It is very nice to sit in a first-class coach. By rights, us horses should go in third-class coaches, for we are dirty and we pong. But who am I to say 'No' to a soft chair?" Then the train started with a lurch and they were on the way to see Luke, the Duke of the dump. The train went faster and faster, and they could see the dump go by in a blur. They saw lots of black smoke from burning boxes. They saw hills of rusty bikes. The large man with a badge served them glasses of coke. It was so nice in Mike's train that they fell asleep. They missed the stop at the church by the strange bridge and the train went speeding on into the night—and Mark still had not had any lunch.

Do you think that Mark's dress needed washing?

au, aw
Do not award ticks for a 'good try'—your pupil will pay for it later!

caught   Paul   hawk   lawn   saw ☐

taught   draw   fawn   thaw   dawn ☐

Paul caught the ball. ☐

I saw a hawk catch some mice on the lawn. ☐

Who taught you how to draw? ☐

At dawn, we saw a deer with her fawn. ☐

Wait for the ice to thaw before you go for a swim. ☐

brawl   fault   paw   because   crawl ☐

launch   prawns   trawl   haul   sprawl ☐

yawn   vault   sauce   jaw   pause ☐

It is not my fault that I got into a brawl! ☐

Joyce likes lots of sauce on her chips. ☐

Our dog could hardly crawl because she hurt her paw. ☐

I like to sprawl across my nice soft bed. ☐

When can we launch the sailboat? ☐

The trawler caught lots of prawns. ☐

Your car will need a hitch if you want to haul a trailer. ☐

I like to have a good yawn when I first wake up. ☐

DECODING POWER PAGE

Some of these words are unusual but they are all real words.

slight	witch	dodge	nigh	☐
saw	Paul	yawn	haul	☐
snatch	dredge	flight	hitch	☐
lawn	fraud	draw	cause	☐
bespoke	uncoil	export	prechill	☐
launch	drawn	claw	fault	☐
spice	first	singe	church	☐
flock	tuck	trike	cake	☐
law	pause	thaw	vault	☐
smudge	bight	retch	cadge	☐
maul	flaw	brawn	taut	☐
nurse	plaice	sir	rage	☐
passes	quilting	sister	stressful	☐
sauce	drawl	raw	haunch	☐

Wordbuilder

If a pupil makes a mistake, back up the cursor and then sound out the word.

fast   fasten   fastened   unfastened   ☐

plore   explore   exploring   ☐

sink   sinkable   unsinkable   ☐

fright   frighten   frightened   ☐

The smart cat unfastened the latch with her paw. ☐

Paul loves to go exploring in strange places. ☐

There is no such thing as an unsinkable ship. ☐

Are you frightened to go into the haunted shack? ☐

block   blocking   unblocking   ☐

flat   flatten   flattened   ☐

light   relight   relighting   ☐

fill   refill   refillable   unrefillable   ☐

sweet   sweeten   sweetened   unsweetened   ☐

I like my hot drinks unsweetened. ☐

Take the matches for relighting the gas cooker. ☐

Is your dad any good at unblocking the drains? ☐

My dad gets his beer in unrefillable kegs. ☐

The coins that fell on the rail were flattened by the train. ☐

> cook, book, look, foot, good, took, what, when, which

You will need a ___ book if you are going to bake a cake.

      camp   cook   crack

When you poke the dog, it will ___ up.

      wash   wake   want

Look what a good ___ Grace is!

      girth   grill   girl

What did Paul put his ___ in?

      foot   fort   fraud

FLUENCY READING

☐ Pass: 10 sec.   ☆ Bonus: 8 sec.   ☆☆ Double Bonus: 6 sec.

bung	bell	tern	serf	☐ ☆ ☆
joint	yarn	chop	zest	☐ ☆ ☆
thank	kiln	gosh	port	☐ ☆ ☆
teen	pork	chink	roar	☐ ☆ ☆
rig	jilt	void	bunch	☐ ☆ ☆
blot	lung	twill	sheer	☐ ☆ ☆

Paul, the Gawky Hawk.

Mark woke up and took a good look at his watch, and he saw that it was ten o'clock. It was a dark night and the train went speeding on. Hank, the hunch-backed horse, was sprawled in his soft chair, snoring in his sleep. Mark gave Hank a poke in the jaw, and then the horse woke up. Mark said, "It is dark and my mum will miss me. By now she will have called the cops. What can we do?" Hank had a good stretch. He had a good yawn. Then he said, "Why, I cannot say what we should do. Hunch-backed horses are not all that bright at night."

Just then, they saw the large man with a badge. He was bringing cokes and some cake to keep them awake. He said, "Say, you have missed your stop. You should have changed trains at the church by the strange bridge. We passed that stop a long way back." Mark asked, "What can we do? I must call my mum, or she might think I have been flattened by a truck." The large man with a badge scratched his shirt, which was still full of mice. "I cannot say," he said, "because I am not that smart, but I will call Paul, the gawky hawk, because he is a very, very smart bird."

The large man with a badge called for Paul, the gawky hawk, who came flying into the coach. Paul landed on the back of a chair and dug his claws into the cloth. "What can I do for you?" he squawked (for he was a hawk). "I am a very, very smart bird, and I can do anything." Mark asked, "Can you tell my mum that I have come to no harm? I think she likes me a lot." Paul the gawky hawk stretched his wing and scratched his maw. "Why not? Is there anything more I can do for you?"

Hank, the hunch-backed horse woke up and said, "How can we get back and change trains at the church by the strange bridge? We need to go and see Luke, the Duke of the dump."

Paul plucked a quill from his tail and picked his teeth, (he was lucky to have teeth because hawks do not have teeth). "Just turn your watch back to seven o'clock. This train stops at the church by the strange bridge at seven." With a smart squawk, Paul went flying off into the next coach.

Do you think that Mark has lost his watch?

Word Search

gawky   are
strange   awe
nicely   ice
light   ply
harpy   tree
truce   jaw
rake   luke

s	t	r	a	n	g	e
i	r	a	w	i	a	c
l	u	k	e	c	w	a
i	c	e	i	e	k	u
g	e	a	p	l	y	s
h	a	r	p	y	n	e
t	r	e	e	j	a	w

-tch, -dge, -igh

If a pupil makes a mistake, back up the cursor and then sound out the word.

budge   Dutch   smudge   slight   night   ☐

flight   lodge   sketch   fudge   fridge   ☐

match   fight   watch   cadge   wedge   ☐

When the match is done, we can watch the fight. ☐

The Dutch boy says he will not budge. ☐

There is a slight smudge on your face. ☐

We took the last flight of the night. ☐

Luke can draw a sketch of the hunting lodge. ☐

Did you put the fudge in the fridge? ☐

patch   stitch   might   nudge   witch   ☐

sledge   hitch   light   switch   bright   ☐

pitch   stretch   dodge   bridge   sight   ☐

Ask Madge to stitch a patch on your shirt. ☐

Give the witch a nudge and she might wake up. ☐

The farmer hitched his horse to the sledge. ☐

Could you switch off the bright lights? ☐

We had to dodge the cars that were crossing the bridge. ☐

They took the player off the football pitch on a stretcher. ☐

DECODING POWER PAGE

Remember to practise the flashcards at least once a day!

jaunt	sawn	yaw	spawn	☐
Wight	clutch	trudge	blight	☐
forge	slurp	farce	swirl	☐
botch	pledge	high	Dutch	☐
jaw	faun	saucer	gawk	☐
snitch	nigh	drudge	crutch	☐
craw	flaunt	prawn	haunt	☐
sigh	midge	crutch	match	☐
Turk	slice	cringe	smirk	☐
distort	restock	bedeck	unspoilt	☐
patch	thigh	sledge	blotch	☐
trawl	paw	taunt	Maud	☐
cake	fluke	spike	woke	☐
glitch	fight	crotch	wedge	☐

Wordbuilder

Always use the cursor!

turn	return	returned	☐
thank	thankful	thankfully	☐
tend	pretend	pretended	☐
dress	undress	undressing	☐

Paul returned from the pub crawl at ten o'clock. ☐

Thankfully, they have shifted all that sludge for us. ☐

The hawk pretended that it had hurt its claw. ☐

Do not watch when I am undressing. ☐

stack	stacking	restacking	☐
serve	served	reserved	☐
plain	explain	explained	☐
play	display	displayed	☐
miss	dismiss	dismissed	☐

Joyce got a job restacking the shelves at the store. ☐

Have you reserved a place for the match tonight? ☐

Mike just explained how to catch a pike. ☐

We were dismissed when we had done a good job. ☐

My best painting is displayed on the board in the hall. ☐

> cook, book, look, foot, good, took, what, when, which

Look what the cat ___ in!

      dragged   quake   sadly

A king, a queen and a duke are all very ___.

      posh   pond   poke

I like to watch my dad when he is ___ the car.

      fishing   fixing   falling

Which ___ will Maud be sailing on the lake?

      book   boast   boat

FLUENCY READING

☐ Pass: 10 sec. ☆ Bonus: 8 sec. ☆ Double Bonus: 6 sec.

bore	foist	still	hoist	☐ ☆ ☆
pram	char	flock	act	☐ ☆ ☆
green	fair	bang	snap	☐ ☆ ☆
grab	hush	flit	perch	☐ ☆ ☆
maths	tor	grass	gait	☐ ☆ ☆
oar	blob	shark	ask	☐ ☆ ☆

Smudge, the Batty Cat.

When Paul, the gawky hawk, had flapped his way into the next coach, Mark said, "I may as well turn back my watch." But he forgot to take some cake from the large man with the badge, so Hank, the hunch-backed horse, scoffed the lot.

When the hands on Mark's watch were set at seven o'clock, the train stopped at the church by the strange bridge. Mark and Hank stepped off the coach into broad daylight. "Why, this is all right," said Hank, "Now we can catch the train that will take us to see Luke, the Duke of the dump." Mark wished he had some lunch. He wished he was with his pal Vern, and he wanted to see Froid, the pet snail. He even wanted a sniff of Bart, the damp dog. But most of all he wanted some shorts and a shirt, because he was fed up with being a girl.

Then they met Smudge, the batty cat who wore a flat cap. Smudge said, "I live in the church by the strange bridge, and I catch lots of nice mice and fat rats. Would you like to meet the mice I have caught? They are very nice." Mark said, "Thank you, but we must be getting on to see Luke, the Duke of the dump. The large man with a badge said that we have to change here." Smudge asked, "What would you like to change into?" Mark said, "I would like to change into a boy right now." "You cannot do that," said Smudge, "for you are a girl. Would you like to change into a witch? Witches can cast spells and I should think they have lots of fun."

But Mark did not want to be a witch. "We just want to change trains," he said. Smudge, the batty cat (who wore a flat cap) said, "Why, you cannot change trains. Even witches cannot change trains into something else." Mark said, "But we must change trains because we are going to see Luke, the Duke of the dump." Smudge said, "Then you had best take a boat and go up the creepy creek that runs under the strange bridge. You can take my boat if you wish."

Do you think Hank can swim?

Silent 'e'

If a pupil makes a mistake, back up the cursor and then sound out the word.

time	home	came	same	hope	smile	☐
game	those	name	rope	safe	cope	☐
late	made	ride	spade	lane	prude	☐
trade	pine	Clive	pile	hide	nude	☐

We all came home at the same time. ☐

What is the name of the game? ☐

I hope you can cope with those ropes. ☐

We were late, but we made it home safely. ☐

I will trade my spade for a ride up the lane. ☐

Clive will hide in that pile of pine logs. ☐

June	shine	stale	date	these	ale	☐
pipe	rude	nine	grapes	pale	wipe	☐
dude	ripe	ate	hole	five	use	☐
stole	Pete	fuse	mole	Jane	zone	☐

That dude was very rude to June. ☐

Wipe that pipe until it shines. ☐

The pale ale is a bit stale. ☐

I ate five ripe grapes and nine of these dates. ☐

The mole stole back into its hole. ☐

Did Pete use the right fuse? ☐

DECODING POWER PAGE

Always use the cursor!

sketch	sludge	light	itch	☐
made	hide	home	June	☐
brawl	vaunt	crawl	haul	☐
these	wide	hope	lane	☐
dawn	taut	gaunt	thaw	☐
cute	mole	safe	wipe	☐
light	grudge	notch	Wight	☐
age	lance	curb	twirl	☐
tube	wise	tame	note	☐
fawn	maul	pawn	auk	☐
shine	tale	stone	mule	☐
batch	pledge	might	fetch	☐
failed	gormless	oaken	vainly	☐
cube	bite	lone	tape	☐

Wordbuilder

Remember to practise the flashcards at least once a day!

take   mistake   mistakable   unmistakable ☐

use   used   unused ☐

time   timed   mistimed ☐

sell   selling   reselling ☐

With your green hair, you are unmistakable. ☐

Could you return your unused books? ☐

We crashed because I mistimed that turn. ☐

Pete made ten quid by reselling that bike. ☐

late   relate   related ☐

ripe   ripen   ripened   unripened ☐

line   lined   unlined ☐

port   report   reporter ☐

quote   quoted   misquoted ☐

Is Clive related to you or is he just a good mate? ☐

Dale mistimed the punch line when telling that joke. ☐

That unripened plum will make you ill. ☐

Jane likes to draw on unlined paper. ☐

The reporter misquoted the speech. ☐

| teach, real, eat, please, year, leave, reach, meat, friend |

Please leave your coats in the ___.

      hitch   hall   hedge

Last year, Clive and Jane gave up eating ___.

      toads   slime   meat

Pete is really keen to ___ your friends.

      meat   meet   cook

Can you ___ the book on the top shelf?

      reach   real   eat

FLUENCY READING

☐ Pass: 10 sec. ☆ Bonus: 8 sec. ☆☆ Double Bonus: 6 sec.

coil	seer	hump	crack	☐ ☆ ☆
woad	chuck	grip	torch	☐ ☆ ☆
tart	pang	more	loach	☐ ☆ ☆
nest	Claire	loin	swig	☐ ☆ ☆
beef	film	hoard	Cain	☐ ☆ ☆
elm	verse	flap	sheer	☐ ☆ ☆

Mastery Test

Any pupil who does not pass this test must go back to page 83. This is very important—a child who is struggling will not be learning. Contrary to what you would think, most children do not mind going back. It's better than getting things wrong.

If the pupil needs to go back, use a different coloured pencil for ticking the boxes.

Timed reading: 'Pass' mark is 15 seconds per line.

rude	lawn	expand	trawler	☐
matches	trade	sauce	prefix	☐
drawing	lighter	hope	fault	☐
hawk	crawled	misjudge	wipe	☐

Reading accuracy: Pass mark is one mistake.

Do not prompt. You may allow the pupil to self correct, but you cannot say anything except "Try again".

Paul hitched up the trailer to haul the junk to the dump. ☐

Clive was late, but he still got home safely. ☐

Jane got up at dawn, and saw the hawk on the lawn. ☐

Pete and June are going to pick grapes in France. ☐

Floyd, the Faultless Fish.

Smudge, the batty cat—who wore a flat cap—took Mark and Hank to the creepy creek, where his boat was parked. "This is a very safe boat," he said, "It is made of the finest pine and it is nine yards long and five feet wide. It is just the right size for a hunch-backed horse." Hank said, "How can we find the way to see Luke, the Duke of the dump?"

Smudge said, "You must meet my mate. His name is Floyd, the faultless fish. He is a good sole and he is very wise. He will take you where you want to go." Then Smudge spotted some cute mice and he went back in the cat-flap in the church by the strange bridge. Hank and Mark got into Smudge's boat and they shook hands with Floyd, the faultless fish. Or they had to pretend to shake hands, because fish do not have hands. "We must go quickly if we want to catch the tide," said Floyd.

Mark cast off the ropes, and Smudge's boat sailed away. The tide in the creepy creek ran quite fast and they had to watch out for barges and whales. Mark had to steer because horses cannot steer boats. They stopped for a while when Floyd met a skate who was his best mate. Hank sat on the oars and watched the water slide by. "This is the life," he said, "I should have been a sailor."

Floyd, the faultless fish, stopped again and scratched his nose. "Eeny, meeny, miny, mo, which way should I go?" he asked, flapping his fin to right and left. "What a shame," he said, "I think we are lost. There are too many creeks in this place and they all look the same." Just then Floyd spotted a pub on the side of the creek. "We must go there and find out where we are," he said.

Mark and Hank got out of the boat and went up the slope to the pub. "I must have a beer," said Hank, "and I must get one for Floyd. I bet he drinks like a fish." But Mark did not want any beer. "What have you got for lunch?" he asked the girl in the pub. "It is too late for a plate of nosh," she said, "But you can have a bag of hedgehog crisps. They are made from fresh road-kill, and they are very nice."

Would you like some hedgehog crisps?

ir, ur, -ce, -ge

Do not award ticks for a 'good try'—your pupil will pay for it later!

prince	dance	chirp	bird	race	☐
office	nice	sage	mince	curly	☐
Turk	plunge	urge	squirt	slurp	☐

The prince asked the fair maiden to go to the dance. ☐

Birds like to chirp in the morning. ☐

I will race you back to the office. ☐

Mince cooked with sage is very nice. ☐

Do Turks have curly hair? ☐

Any time you get the urge, just plunge into the lake. ☐

purse	birth	plaice	sauce	surf	☐
chance	wage	nurse	spruce	huge	☐
dirty	barge	bilge	range	firm	☐

My sister gave Marge a purse for her birthday. ☐

Do you like sauce with your plaice and chips? ☐

This is your last chance to ride a surfboard. ☐

Do nurses get paid a good wage? ☐

We sat next to the huge spruce tree. ☐

The bilges of a barge are full of dirty water. ☐

DECODING ⚡ POWER ⚡ PAGE

Remember to practise the flashcards at least once a day!

date	life	hole	fuse	☐
plunge	murk	chance	birth	☐
witch	dodge	right	badge	☐
urn	sage	flirt	face	☐
jaw	awl	gauze	sauce	☐
frailest	reborn	porky	belong	☐
same	side	bone	theme	☐
daub	law	cause	Paul	☐
hinge	lurk	race	shirt	☐
switch	fudge	night	hedge	☐
irk	dice	burp	bilge	☐
Pete	rise	pale	prune	☐
paw	fraud	bawl	taunt	☐
purse	wage	voice	dirt	☐

Wordbuilder

| Always use the cursor! |

pute	dispute	disputed	undisputed	☐
want	wanted	unwanted		☐
float	floated	refloated		☐
charge	charged	recharged		☐

My darts team is the undisputed winner of the match. ☐

Please leave all your unwanted books here. ☐

After my boat sank, the divers refloated it. ☐

Dad just recharged his cordless drill. ☐

friend	friendly	unfriendly	☐
place	replace	replacement	☐
turn	return	returning	☐
slice	sliced	unsliced	☐
place	placed	misplaced	☐

I have not lost my glasses, I have just misplaced them. ☐

Do you think that dog is unfriendly? ☐

Paul wants me to get an unsliced loaf at the shop. ☐

Joyce and Maud will be returning at nine o'clock. ☐

If that shirt is no good, we will give you a replacement. ☐

teach, real, eat, please, year, leave, reach, meat, friend

When can we leave this boring ___?

        plaice   place   please

My friend will teach you how to ___ meat.

        road   roach   roast

Can you reach the light.___?

        switch   swift   swirl

I did not mean to ___ all the meat.

        ask   eat   end

FLUENCY READING

☐ Pass: 10 sec.   ☆ Bonus: 8 sec.   ☆☆ Double Bonus: 6 sec.

foil	aft	chit	fret	☐ ☆☆
core	goad	bank	quilt	☐ ☆☆
inch	plum	tosh	quench	☐ ☆☆
loft	shack	brass	pair	☐ ☆☆
shore	baize	pond	quench	☐ ☆☆
spot	deer	tee	mint	☐ ☆☆

Beer at Dawn's.

Hank, the hunch-backed horse, took a large pail of beer and went off to soak it up with Floyd, the faultless fish. The girl in the pub said to Mark, "You should try hedgehog crisps, because they are made from fresh road-kill. They are very nice when you wash them down with a glass of dirty ditch water." Mark said, "Thank you, but I don't want hedgehog crisps. Hedgehogs have sharp quills and one might get stuck in my throat."

The girl in the pub wiped down the bar with a grubby rag and slurped down a glass of white wine. She said, "My name is Dawn. They call me Dawn because I can talk until dawn, or until you start to yawn, whichever comes first. But I like you because you are a very cute girl."

Mark said, "But I am not a girl. If I ever find Luke, the Duke of the dump, then I will get a job. Then I can get a loan from Mike, the loan shark, and then I can get a pair of shorts and a shirt from Groan, the croaking toad. Then you will see that I am a boy." Dawn said, "Your dress is very dirty. When you live in a dump, dresses get dirty very quickly. You will never get a job in a dirty dress. Give it to me and I will wash it for you. Put on this green bathrobe and I will rinse the grime and sludge from your frock."

Just then, Hank, the hunch-backed horse, came back and said, "I must help Floyd, the faultless fish. A man just came in and asked for fish and chips. Floyd is legless, for he is a fish. I must help him get away." Mark said, "I cannot go because this bathrobe belongs to Dawn, the barmaid, and she is washing my dress. What can we do?"

Do you think Hank paid for his beer?

Silent 'e'

If a pupil makes a mistake, back up the cursor and then sound out the word.

Clive	jade	wrote	note	bike	tube	☐
Jane	mine	robe	white	stone	prune	☐
those	bite	make	fine	gate	pine	☐

Jade wrote a note to Clive. ☐

Do not bite hard on those prunes—they have stones. ☐

I will make the gate with the finest pine. ☐

Jane had to patch the tube on her bike. ☐

The white bath robe is mine. ☐

skate	ice	rode	hate	quite	mate	☐
Pete	home	late	rule	wife	Clive	☐
make	bone	shame	alone	tales	Jane	☐
sale	crate	these	wine	style	froze	☐

Pete rode home quite late last night. ☐

Clive's wife makes all the rules at home. ☐

My mate hates to skate on thin ice. ☐

Leave the dog alone with his bone. ☐

It's a shame that Jane is telling tales. ☐

These crates of wine are on sale. ☐

131

DECODING POWER PAGE

Some of these words are unusual but they are all real words.

pace	birch	lunge	furl	☐
late	mile	rule	rode	☐
fault	trawl	Maud	raw	☐
quote	pipe	line	sale	☐
notch	sight	clutch	cadge	☐
tune	quite	name	scope	☐
fleece	spurt	ice	chirp	☐
saw	faun	drawn	vaunt	☐
time	use	flame	cope	☐
unaided	exactly	precast	disbanding	☐
ate	Clive	pole	rude	☐
verge	lurch	force	quirk	☐
gauze	flaw	pawn	haunt	☐
hate	dude	robe	swipe	☐

Wordbuilder

> Do not award ticks for a 'good try'—your pupil will pay for it later!

firm   confirm   confirmed   unconfirmed ☐

play   played   misplayed ☐

part   depart   departing ☐

light   delight   delighted ☐

port   report   reports ☐

We have unconfirmed reports of a space-ship landing. ☐

We lost because the goal-keeper misplayed the ball. ☐

I will be delighted to see my friends again. ☐

The train to Dover will be departing at nine o'clock. ☐

wise   unwise   unwisely ☐

change   changed   unchanged ☐

give   forgive   forgiven ☐

fess   confess   confessed ☐

skill   skilful   skilfully ☐

Small boys and girls sometimes act unwisely. ☐

The score is still unchanged. ☐

Jane plays the game very skilfully. ☐

You will be forgiven if you have confessed your crime. ☐

teach, real, eat, please, year, leave, reach, meat, friend

His hair is not ___ , he has a wig!

        rich   real   ring

Did you see where he put his glass of ___?

        been   beet   beer

When will we be eating that ___ of beef?

        join   joist   joint

My dad has been a joiner for ten ___ .

        yours   years   yeast

FLUENCY READING

☐ Pass: 10 sec. ☆ Bonus: 8 sec. ☆☆ Double Bonus: 6 sec.

pick	swam	oar	noise	☐ ☆ ☆
spot	tall	bunk	hotly	☐ ☆ ☆
sleet	ball	plum	running	☐ ☆ ☆
float	hall	quest	taller	☐ ☆ ☆
flair	fall	snail	hitting	☐ ☆ ☆
horn	flatly	snack	small	☐ ☆ ☆

Maud, the Maudlin Trawler-Woman.

Hank, the hunch-backed horse, launched the boat that belonged to Smudge, the batty cat with the flat cap. He had to save Floyd, the faultless fish, from a grim fate. Mark waved as they sailed away, and then he went back into the pub and sat next to the coal burning in the grate. Dawn, the girl in the pub, was washing his dress. He really wanted something to eat—anything but hedgehog crisps. Or fish and chips.

Dawn came back and said, "Now your dress is clean and when it is dry you can get a job. I will talk to Maud, the maudlin trawler-woman. She might give you a job trawling for small prawns." Dawn hung Mark's dress to dry by the flames, and she went off to find Maud, the maudlin trawler-woman.

After a while, a big woman with a wooden nose came stomping into the pub. "My name is Maud," she said, "and I am the maudlin trawler-woman. I may cry a lot but I catch the best small prawns in this dump. If you want a job on my trawler, you must pretend to be a boy. I do not give jobs to small girls." Mark said, "I will do my best. I will pretend that my dress is really a shirt and a pair of shorts. And I will cry a lot, because I do need some lunch."

Dawn yawned as she gave Maud a glass of beer. She winked at Mark and said, "You really are a good girl. I bet you will catch lots of small prawns, and you will cry a lot." So Maud drank her beer and took Mark down to her trawler.

Do you think Mark likes prawns?

au, au

If a pupil makes a mistake, back up the cursor and then sound out the word.

Maud	drawn	because	haunt	brawn	☐
hawk	claw	dawn	crawl	pause	☐
sawn	fraud	daub	maul	sprawl	☐

Maud took a ride in a horse-drawn cart. ☐

No one will go in those woods because they are haunted. ☐

This job takes brains, not brawn. ☐

Hawks have very sharp claws. ☐

Dawn had to crawl under the fence. ☐

Shall we pause for a cup of tea? ☐

Paul	vault	Saul	caught	prawn	☐
taught	brawl	jaw	yawn	Paul	☐
dawn	gaunt	drawn	jaunt	sauce	☐

Paul keeps his cash safe in a bank vault. ☐

Maud caught her sleeve on a rose bush. ☐

Who taught you how to catch prawns? ☐

Roy broke his jaw in a brawl. ☐

Paul woke up at dawn and had a good yawn. ☐

Saul looked gaunt and drawn after being so ill. ☐

DECODING ~ POWER ~ PAGE

Do not award ticks for a 'good try'—your pupil will pay for it later!

mate	pine	cute	zone	☐
drawl	pause	claw	gaunt	☐
change	bird	lace	hurt	☐
draw	haunt	Gaul	prawn	☐
edge	bight	catch	smudge	☐
sawn	craw	daub	sauce	☐
retrain	because	unhinge	exerting	☐
slide	gale	Eve	those	☐
caught	crawl	Maud	yawn	☐
mince	flange	burnt	sir	☐
dawn	haunch	gawk	taught	☐
ride	stale	trim	drove	☐
prejudge	distance	switches	burning	☐
lawn	saucer	faun	brawn	☐

Wordbuilder

Remember to practise the flashcards at least once a day!

daunt	daunted	undaunted	☐
hope	hopeless	hopelessly	☐
pect	expect	expected	unexpected	☐
mark	remark	remarkable	☐
dress	address	addressed	☐

The ship sailed on, undaunted by the storm. ☐

We got hopelessly lost when Paul mislaid the map. ☐

Maud's return last night was unexpected. ☐

Floyd scored a remarkable goal in the match today. ☐

That letter is addressed to Dawn. ☐

ply	apply	applying	☐
watch	watchable	unwatchable	☐
stand	understand	understanding	☐
fish	fisher	fisherman	☐

Spike is applying for a job at the chip shop. ☐

That film is so bad that it is unwatchable. ☐

I like my teacher because she is very understanding. ☐

The fisherman caught five roach, a perch and a pike. ☐

> teach, real, eat, please, year, leave, reach, meat, friend

I really want to go flying to ___.

        Spain   sport   spoil

Please leave your seat when the play comes to an ___.

        end   eat   eke

Can we all play football in that ___?

        yard   yank   year

I found out about this place from my best ___.

        freeze   friend   forge

FLUENCY READING

☐ Pass: 10 sec.   ☆ Bonus: 8 sec.   ★ Double Bonus: 6 sec.

scar	asking	grill	cutter	☐ ☆ ★
jolt	helped	score	nipper	☐ ☆ ★
spoil	lastly	scorch	calling	☐ ☆ ★
harmless	hoist	playful	rubbed	☐ ☆ ★
steep	hottest	queer	sharpen	☐ ☆ ★
boxer	creel	fattest	landing	☐ ☆ ★

Mark's Dream.

Mark went back down to the creek with Maud, the maudlin trawler-woman. Hank, the hunch-backed horse, was not there, and the boat that belonged to Smudge, the batty cat in a flat cap, was gone. Floyd, the faultless fish, was nowhere to be seen and Mark hoped that he was not sitting on a plate of chips. Mark felt very sleepy when he boarded Maud's trawler. He fell asleep on a pile of ropes right away.

Mark had some strange dreams. First, Bart, the junk-yard dog, took a loaf and some milk to his mum. His mum seemed to think that Bart was her son and she said, "Thank you, Mark. You are a good dog, but you took ever such a long time." Mark was cross because his mum would not look at him and she stroked Bart's damp fur. Then Froid, the pet snail, came in and he was huge. His shell was painted with green letters that said "For sale". Vern was with him, but he was very small, and he was sitting in Froid's chair. Vern said, "You must go to see Groan, the croaking toad. He wants to sell you a shirt and a pair of shorts. He said that he will sell them very cheaply, and then you can be a boy again."

Next, Groyne, the grey-green goat, who wore his hair in a quiff, turned up and said, "Herb, the sharp shark, is waiting for

you with his bus pass. He will take you to see Jake, the fake snake. Have a chomp on this lovely tin foil." Mark went down to the road and got on the bus. The driver was Mike, the loan shark, who sat next to his friend Patch, the pointless pike. Jake, the fake snake, had become a real snake but he was still missing one of his trainers.

The large man with a badge walked in and said, "This bus will not start. You will have to push it all the way to the tip." So Mark left his seat and got behind the bus. He pushed it as hard as he could but it would not budge. His feet were sinking deeper and deeper into the moist muck, he sank down to his thighs until his legs were stuck. Then Paul, the gawky hawk, landed on his back and squawked, "Push harder! Push harder!" Mark yelled, "Please help me!" Then he woke up and saw Maud, the maudlin trawler-woman, standing next to him. She said, "You just missed lunch because you were sleeping, but now you can go down and help wash the dirty dishes."

Do you think Mark will be a good fisherman?

Silent 'e'

Always use the cursor!

bride	white	Jade	skate	blade	close	☐
twine	gate	scone	stale	trade	game	☐
style	robe	cute	late	side	shape	☐

The bride was dressed in white. ☐

Jade should sharpen the blades on her skates. ☐

I will trade my scone for your stale cakes. ☐

Those cute robes are all in the latest style. ☐

Our side must get into shape for the next game. ☐

Do not forget to close the gate and fasten in with twine. ☐

pipes	froz	broke	quite	blame	crime	☐
shame	Pete	ate	cube	flame	close	☐
wise	nine	rise	slope	ice	slide	☐

Those pipes just froze because our heater broke down. ☐

I am not quite sure who to blame for the crime. ☐

It is a shame that Pete ate all the sugar cubes. ☐

Are you sure it is wise to sit so close to the flames? ☐

The sun will rise at nine this morning. ☐

You cannot slide down the slope if there is no ice on it. ☐

DECODING POWER PAGE

Remember to practise the flashcards at least once a day!

launch	fawn	spawn	yaw	☐
nude	stem	stole	dive	☐
Bruce	surf	merge	quirt	☐
shape	crime	rope	shun	☐
Dutch	trudge	slight	botch	☐
flit	crude	gripe	shame	☐
boarder	tuneful	aired	charmless	☐
midge	blight	switch	budge	☐
Jade	ripe	shed	game	☐
bright	hutch	wedge	ketch	☐
stab	dime	mine	cone	☐
hawk	daub	paw	yawn	☐
reserve	patches	bewitch	flirting	☐
Crete	shade	mine	slope	☐

Wordbuilder

If a pupil makes a mistake, back up the cursor and then sound out the word.

play   replay   replayed   ☐

point   appoint   disappoint   disappointing   ☐

force   enforce   enforcement   ☐

card   discard   discarded   ☐

How many times have they replayed that tune?   ☐

Gail's grades were disappointing.   ☐

Law enforcement is a cop's main job.   ☐

We had to pick up all the discarded cans.   ☐

part   depart   department   ☐

help   helpless helplessly   ☐

plain   explain   explained   ☐

ploy   employ   employed   unemployed   ☐

use   useless   ☐

My mum likes to go shopping in big department stores.   ☐

Paul looked on helplessly as his toy boat sank.   ☐

Our teacher has explained that twice so far.   ☐

Jake got a job after he had been unemployed for a year.   ☐

It is useless trying to explain that to my sister.   ☐

> out, found, our, loud, house, about, sure, sugar

My shirt has got some dirt on the ___.

      slipper   sleeve   sleep

Our house is not very ___.

      large   purge   slur

Did you let the bird out of its ___?

      cake   curd   cage

Are you sure Dad has found out about our ___ speakers.

      loud   launch   sugar

FLUENCY READING

☐ Pass: 10 sec.   ☆ Bonus: 8 sec.   ★ Double Bonus: 6 sec.

smallest	badly	float	musty	☐ ☆ ★
helpful	harder	happy	sneer	☐ ☆ ★
scar	glasses	oar	sticky	☐ ☆ ★
hike	queer	stoke	happen	☐ ☆ ★
wilful	spoilt	Jake	catty	☐ ☆ ★
stair	bike	thinnest	flip	☐ ☆ ★

Mastery Test

Any pupil who does not pass this test must go back to page 122. This is very important—a child who is struggling will not be learning. Contrary to what you would think, most children do not mind going back. It's better than getting things wrong.

If the pupil needs to go back, use a different coloured pencil for ticking the boxes.

Timed reading: 'Pass' mark is 15 seconds per line.

sprawl	swine	burning	between	☐
tallest	sawn	slope	switches	☐
handful	bosses	taught	cute	☐
bride	cutter	sunken	fraud	☐

Reading accuracy: Pass mark is one mistake.
Do not prompt. You may allow the pupil to self correct, but you cannot say anything except "Try again".

Our pipes were frozen when the heater was broken. ☐

June and Clive had to crawl under the fence. ☐

Maud and Paul caught nine large prawns. ☐

Pete and Jade are getting into shape for the big game. ☐

Nate, the First Mate.

Maud, the maudlin trawler-woman, said to Mark, "You must go below and help wash the dishes. Just dive down that hatch and you will find the mess decks. That is where the dirty dishes are." Mark ran down the deck and went below, but he could not find the mess decks. Then he bumped into a large, smelly dog who barked, "Watch where you are going, little girl. I am Nate, the first mate, and I am a sea dog from way back. When Maud is sleeping, I am in charge of this trawler." With that, Nate took a puff on his pipe, and a huge cloud of smoke came out his ears.

Mark said, "Please Sir, I must find the mess decks. Maud said that I should help wash the dirty dishes. But you should not smoke that pipe because it is bad for you." Nate, the first mate said, "Why, sea dogs must smoke pipes. It is in the rule book. Here, come and look and you will see that I am right." Nate led Mark to the deck house, and then up to the bridge. The bridge is where they steer a ship, and on the bridge of the trawler Mark saw that they were out to sea. He could not see the dump anywhere—there was water as far as he could see.

Nate, the first mate got out the rule book, and Mark saw that he was right: sea dogs must smoke pipes. Then Nate said,

"I have been a sea dog for all my life. Ever since I was a pup I have sailed the seven seas. I have seen many strange sights, and I have seen lamp-posts in many strange lands. I have done so many things that are bad for dogs that smoking a pipe hardly matters." Mark asked, "Please Sir, do you think I could have some lunch?" Nate said, "Why yes you can. You can have what is left in this can of dog food."

Mark looked in the can of dog food and he felt sick. It was full of slime and rotten meat. He said, "Please Sir, can you tell me how to get to the mess decks? Maud will be very cross if I do not help wash the dirty dishes."

Do you think Nate should clean his teeth?

ue, ew

If a pupil makes a mistake, back up the cursor and then sound out the word.

Sue	knew	cruel	crew	flew	clue	☐
new	blue	Kew	few	glue	threw	☐
stew	glue	screw	fuel	yew	value	☐

Sue knew that she was being cruel. ☐

The crew flew the new plane over Kew. ☐

Paul drew a few lines in blue paint. ☐

Joyce threw the rotten stew in the bin. ☐

Drew fixed the board with glue and screws. ☐

You can burn those yew logs—they are very good fuel. ☐

true	grew	pew	blue	brew	flue	☐
argue	knew	sue	newt	due	chew	☐
shrew	hue	dew	clue	skew	duel	☐

Is it true that Pete grew five inches last year? ☐

Some blue smoke went up the flue. ☐

Sit in that pew while I brew some tea. ☐

I think he knew when Sue was due back. ☐

A newt cannot chew because it has no teeth. ☐

Never argue with your teacher—it will get you disliked. ☐

DECODING POWER PAGE

Do not award ticks for a 'good try'—your pupil will pay for it later!

pope	trade	five	came	☐
blue	few	yew	stew	☐
auburn	awful	saunter	shawl	☐
Kew	clue	new	Sue	☐
page	skirmish	lice	turf	☐
drew	flew	brew	rue	☐
grip	slime	Luke	ode	☐
kitchen	lodge	fright	scotch	☐
mew	true	newt	glue	☐
launder	tawny	applaud	drawn	☐
fuel	skew	hue	grew	☐
plate	flit	wife	rule	☐
unloader	explode	disgrace	predate	☐
due	chew	pew	flue	☐

Wordbuilder

Always use the cursor!

harm	harmless	harmlessly	☐
fright	frighten	frightening	☐
grace	disgrace	disgraceful	☐
tain	contain	container	☐

The bomb dropped harmlessly into the sea. ☐

Sue won't watch that film because it is too frightening. ☐

Our dog did something disgraceful on the carpet. ☐

You should keep those shells in a steel container. ☐

norm	normal	normally	☐
agree	disagree	disagreement	☐
joy	enjoy	enjoyable	☐
fess	confess	confessed	☐
heat	reheat	reheated	☐

Jane normally gets out of bed at six o'clock. ☐

Floyd had a disagreement with his teacher. ☐

Joyce had a most enjoyable time at the fair. ☐

Paul confessed that he swiped my lighter. ☐

Dawn has just reheated the stew for lunch. ☐

> out, found, our, loud, house, about, sure, sugar

Are you sure you saw him twice last ___?

    weed   weep   week

Have you found the rice I left at your ___?

    burr   blurt   house

The men digging up the road found the burst ___ main.

    water   merger   furl

How much do they charge for a large bag of ___?

    church   price   sugar

FLUENCY READING

☐ Pass: 10 sec.   ☆ Bonus: 8 sec.   ✯ Double Bonus: 6 sec.

brick	bloater	luck	backless	☐ ☆ ✯
needed	neck	store	kick	☐ ☆ ✯
muck	classes	twain	quack	☐ ☆ ✯
gloat	nuke	torches	snake	☐ ☆ ✯
call	hoard	Luke	thickest	☐ ☆ ✯
chicken	joist	bloke	bashful	☐ ☆ ✯

Sue, the Gruesome Stoker.

Nate, the first mate, puffed on his pipe and said, "If Maud wants you to wash the dirty dishes, you had better go and do just that. Nobody messes with Maudlin Maud, not when she has been crying into her beer." So Mark came down from the bridge, and he kept going down hatches. He found himself down in the bilges of the trawler. It was very hot below because there was black coal burning in the boilers.

Then a loud voice said, "Who are you? My name is Sue. I am Sue, the gruesome stoker. I have a steel ring in my nose, and a blue tattoo on my arm. This is a hard crew and I am the hardest of the lot. We do not need little girls on this trawler."

"My name is Mark and I really am a boy," Mark said. "Maud said that I should help wash the dirty dishes but I cannot find the mess decks. What should I do?" Sue, the gruesome stoker, said, "Why, you can help me stoke the boilers. If there is no steam in the boilers, the screw will not turn and then this trawler will not trawl. Pick up that shovel and help me sling coal on the flames."

So Mark picked up the shovel but it was as big as he was, for he was just a small boy. He could not sling coal as well as

Sue, the gruesome stoker. She had big beefy arms and she was very strong. She smelled a bit strong, too. The smoke from the burning coal got up Mark's nose and made him sneeze. He was not sure that he liked his new job. Besides, his dress was getting dirty again.

At last Sue said, "That is just fine for now. The boiler is hot and full of steam. Now we can stop and brew a nice cup of tea." Mark asked, "Why do they call you the gruesome stoker?" Sue said, "Well when I was a girl, I was very big. When my dad came home from trawling, he would say, 'Why Sue, I think you grew some. You must be seven feet tall!' "

The tea was so strong that Mark had to put six lumps of sugar in it. It was so strong that Mark had to chew on it. When Sue was not looking, he tipped it down his socks. The tea was so hot that he started hopping up and down. Sue roared with mirth—"I have never seen such a funny girl," she said. "I think I will keep you here. You are fun to watch!"

What do you think Sue's tattoo looked like?

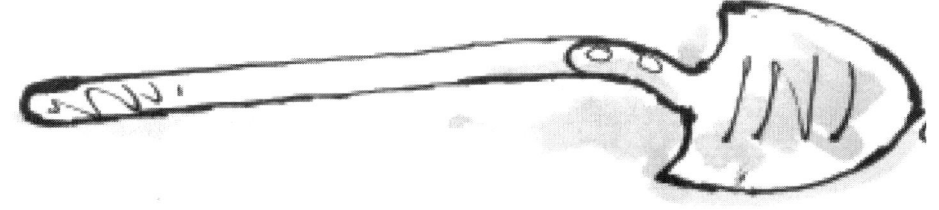

Three-letter Blends

If a pupil makes a mistake, back up the cursor and then sound out the word.

three	stray	shrub	stroll	street	☐
shrimp	squid	thrash	splash	scream	☐
throat	spring	sprout	sprawl	threw	☐

I can see three stray dogs in the shrubs. ☐

Let's take a stroll down the street. ☐

The fisherman caught some shrimp and a squid. ☐

Please do not thrash and splash in the bath. ☐

You can't scream if you have a sore throat. ☐

In the spring, all the seeds will sprout. ☐

scruff	straw	stress	strain	spruce	☐
string	screw	squeak	shrunk	squall	☐
scrap	squall	thrift	splice	scrape	☐

Our scruffy dog sleeps on a pile of straw. ☐

I can't stand all this stress and strain. ☐

Why is my string hanging from the spruce tree? ☐

Put some oil on the screw and it will not squeak. ☐

My jumper shrunk when I got caught in the rain squall. ☐

Our chickens squawk when we feed them the scraps. ☐

DECODING POWER PAGE

Some of these words are unusual but they are all real words.

hew	argue	cue	slew	☐
street	throne	shrub	thrill	☐
scrape	grill	strive	grate	☐
split	screed	strip	scrimp	☐
scrawl	straw	paunch	August	☐
stretch	scram	throb	spruce	☐
gruel	Jew	trews	value	☐
churn	stage	squirt	quince	☐
thrash	squeeze	strut	splint	☐
sprite	throve	shrine	astute	☐
squint	three	shred	thrip	☐
skewer	spew	duel	blue	☐
ketch	splodge	tight	scratch	☐
shrimp	spring	splatter	scruffy	☐

Wordbuilder

Always use the cursor!

cord   record   recorder ☐

agree   agreeable   disagreeable ☐

zip   unzip   unzipped ☐

vent   event   eventful   eventfully   uneventfully ☐

Maud taught us how to play the recorder. ☐

There is no need to be disagreeable about this. ☐

The day passed uneventfully and we were all bored. ☐

It was so hot that Roy unzipped his coat. ☐

arm   armed   disarmed ☐

cuse   excuse   excused ☐

tract   retract   retractable ☐

match   matched   mismatched ☐

place   replace   replacement ☐

The cops disarmed the bank robbers. ☐

We were excused games because it was freezing outside. ☐

My dad has a knife with a retractable blade. ☐

Jake wore mismatched socks today. ☐

If that torch is no good, you should ask for a replacement.☐

out, found, our, loud, house, about, sure, sugar

Did it hurt when I twisted your ___?

    urge   fur   arm

We got a very good price for our ___.

    curve   hue   house

She is sure to need a brace on her ___.

    teen   teeth   three

If you tell a big fib, you are sure to be found ___.

    out   our   oat

FLUENCY READING

☐ Pass: 10 sec. ☆ Bonus: 8 sec. ☆ Double Bonus: 6 sec.

ball	eke	helpless	green	☐ ☆ ☆
predict	wall	unseen	wake	☐ ☆ ☆
hack	joint	unjust	broke	☐ ☆ ☆
explain	drake	unpick	boxes	☐ ☆ ☆
shore	unfit	daft	reject	☐ ☆ ☆
pluck	coast	prevent	Mike	☐ ☆ ☆

Neal, the Real Seal.

Mark did not want to stay in the boiler room with Sue, the gruesome stoker. It was hot and dirty in the boiler room and coal dust got up his nose. So he said to Sue, "I cannot shift coal with tea in my socks, so I must go and find a pair that are clean and dry." Sue said, "That is just fine but make sure you come back quickly. It is time to stoke the flames with more coal or the boiler will run out of steam and this trawler will not go."

So Mark ran up the stairs to the next deck. He ran up more steps until he reached the fresh air. There on deck he tripped over a pail of raw prawns. "Watch out," a voice barked, "Small girls should look where they are going. I am Neal, the real seal, and I am in charge of sorting raw prawns." Mark said, "I am a small boy and I must find the mess decks or Maud, the maudlin trawler-woman, will be cross with me. I should be washing the dirty dishes. Can you tell me how I can find the mess decks?"

Neal, the real seal, said, "By now Maud is crying into her beer again, so you can help me sort prawns. You must put the small prawns in this pail and the large prawns go in that pail."

Mark asked, "What do you do with the small raw prawns?" Neal said, "I eat them because real seals need lots of prawns. They are very nice." "Then what do you do with the large raw prawns?" Mark asked. "Why, I eat those too. A seal can never have too many raw prawns. Now give us a hand sorting prawns."

So Mark sat down and started sorting prawns. Raw prawns do not smell very nice, nor do seals smell so good. But it

was better than shifting coal with Sue, the gruesome stoker. When he had sorted out his first pail of raw prawns, Neal the real seal tipped it into his mouth and ate them in one gulp. "Now that was just fine," said Neal, smacking his lips. "You sure can sort out a nice pail of prawns."

Mark asked, "Why do they call you a real seal? Are there many fake seals about?" Neal looked at Mark shrewdly. "There are lots of fake seals. Seals are very cute, so everyone wants to be a seal. No one will like you if you are cruel to a cute seal. But we can't have fake seals eating all the raw prawns." Then Neal looked around and said, "I can see dark clouds to the west. There is a squall coming. We must put these prawns away and close the hatches. We do not want this trawler to sink in a storm."

Do you think Mark's socks are dry?

Silent 'e'

Do not award ticks for a 'good try'—your pupil will pay for it later!

hope	those	ride	theme	write	nine	☐
lines	slate	blade	knife	twine	plane	☐
state	chime	tune	spine	slide	Pete	☐

I hope we can go on those rides at the theme park. ☐

You must write nine lines on the slate. ☐

Sharpen the blade of the knife and it will cut the twine. ☐

I would not fly on a plane that is in such a bad state. ☐

Those chimes play a nice tune. ☐

Pete hurt his spine going down the slide. ☐

Crete	globe	Jane	like	glide	ice	☐
skate	mule	tame	smile	grade	Dane	☐
nude	cone	scope	drape	gripe	gale	☐

Can you find Crete on the globe? ☐

Jane likes to glide across the ice on her new skates. ☐

I think that mule is tame. ☐

Smile if you got good grades! ☐

Do Danes like to swim in the nude? ☐

Would you like an ice cream cone? ☐

DECODING POWER PAGE

Remember to practise the flashcards at least once a day!

thwack	scrumpy	splutter	strapless	☐
male	bemuse	skate	spiteful	☐
dewy	cruelly	fewer	strew	☐
preclude	dislike	shrunken	scrunches	☐
awe	staunchly	redrawn	gauntest	☐
expose	became	wisely	useful	☐
stripe	preshrunk	thrip	splitting	☐
awning	maudlin	defraud	dawned	☐
prideful	unsafe	shameless	unmade	☐
Tuesday	strew	hewn	clueless	☐
Jane	wifely	beginning	exclude	☐
thwaite	sprayed	thrush	sprightly	☐
bulge	brace	squirl	grunge	☐
unfailing	smartly	prepay	throaty	☐

Wordbuilder

Always use the cursor!

pair	repair	repaired	☐
spot	spotless	spotlessly	☐
screw	unscrew	unscrewed	☐
card	discard	discarded	☐

I just had my watch-strap repaired, but it broke again. ☐

When Joyce has cleaned the house, it will be spotless. ☐

Mike unscrewed the lid on the jar. ☐

Pete discarded all that useless junk. ☐

spell	spelling	misspelling	misspellings	☐
plode	explode	exploded	unexploded	☐
main	remain	remaining		☐
join	joining	adjoining		☐
force	forceful	forcefully		☐

Jane was unhappy about all her misspellings. ☐

You must stay away from that unexploded bomb. ☐

There are just six sweets remaining in the jar. ☐

Dawn and Maud slept in adjoining rooms. ☐

Floyd made his point very forcefully at the meeting. ☐

> old, cold, hold, both, most, were, once, only

We both caught our ___ from Dawn.

      cokes   colds   cones

Most of our friends ___ where we were.

      knew   new   grew

Paul and Joyce were both ___ in the crash.

      hurt   hurry   happy

I like to watch the snakes crawl in the ___.

      bed   grass   stew

FLUENCY READING

☐ Pass: 10 sec.   ☆ Bonus: 8 sec.   ✪ Double Bonus: 6 sec.

expel	thankful	between	joined	☐ ☆ ✪
refrain	catch	quick	judge	☐ ☆ ✪
fridge	flake	tight	unwell	☐ ☆ ✪
play	itch	begin	hedge	☐ ☆ ✪
rake	high	needful	might	☐ ☆ ✪
lodge	display	all	light	☐ ☆ ✪

The Storm.

Up on the bridge, Nate, the first mate blew a mighty blast on his horn, and the crew of the trawler came running out on deck. The black clouds in the west were drawing closer and the sky grew very dark. The crew were stuffing raw prawns in lockers and coiling up all the ropes. They were folding up deckchairs and reeling in the washing lines. Mark did not have a clue what to do. Neal, the real seal was barking out orders to the crew when the first drops of rain fell. A cold wind blew in from the west and Mark was cold, wet and dirty. He was still black with coal dust. "At least this rain will rinse me clean," he said to himself.

Then the squall struck and the wind tore the sea into a white froth. Huge waves tossed the trawler around and Mark had to hold on tight to the rail. Should he go down to the boiler room and help Sue, the gruesome stoker? At least he would not be cold there. But what if the trawler sank? Mark did not want to be trapped down below.

Then Neal, the real seal came up from behind and slapped his back with a flipper. "Come with me, my girl, you will be safe on the bridge. Even if this rusty old trawler sinks, you can hold on to me, for seals can swim very well."

So Mark went with Neal, the real seal up to the bridge. The trawler pitched and rolled and Mark almost lost his grip. A huge wave almost swept him into the sea but Neal saved him just in time. Neal still smelled of raw prawns but Mark held on to him just the same.

Up on the bridge, Maud was still crying, but she had no beer for a change. Nate, the first mate, clung to the wheel and steered the rusty old trawler up and down the huge waves. Nate barked orders to the crew, as only an old sea-dog can. He had drained the water from his pipe and was trying to light it, but no smoke came from his ears. Neal, the real seal, said to Mark, "Now you can be a real sailor. The port lookout has just turned green. Go and be lookout for him. If you see anything but water, you must report it to me."

Do you think Mark will ever get used to raw prawns?

ue, ew
Always use the cursor!

shrew	chew	Sue	blew	jewel	☐
Kew	true	yew	value	knew	☐
clue	dew	new	Lew	cue	☐

Can a shrew chew hard cheese? ☐

The wind blew Sue's boat back to shore. ☐

How many yew trees did you count at Kew Gardens? ☐

What is the true value of these jewels? ☐

I knew that Lew would not have a clue. ☐

There was some dew on the new grass this morning. ☐

threw	screw	blue	gruel	Sue	☐
fluent	Lew	glue	drew	few	☐
crew	cruel	grew	flue	due	☐

Nate threw a few screws into the blue tin. ☐

We had to eat some thin gruel for lunch. ☐

Sue can speak French fluently. ☐

Lew drew a few sketches. ☐

The crew grew restless waiting for the tide. ☐

It is cruel to put glue in the locks. ☐

DECODING POWER PAGE

Do not award ticks for a 'good try'—your pupil will pay for it later!

broadly	cloying	bestir	refloat	☐
screw	newest	shrewd	clue	☐
shrill	squawk	strap	thresh	☐
unwise	brainy	expertly	dismay	☐
thaw	redrawn	tawdry	awning	☐
strewing	airless	doleful	audit	☐
ensue	hoarding	straining	slightly	☐
screed	before	boastful	chewing	☐
painless	shrew	awe	flaunted	☐
cheese	brightest	hugely	drunken	☐
switching	skirmish	bewilder	murky	☐
enrage	curly	darkest	gravely	☐
ewe	rice	sorely	flightless	☐
script	throbbing	bespoke	spawn	☐

Wordbuilder

| Remember to practise the flashcards at least once a day! |

reck	reckless	recklessly	☐
plug	unplug	unplugged	☐
lax	relax	relaxing	☐
mand	demand	demanded	☐

Boy racers like to drive recklessly. ☐

Be sure the toaster is unplugged before you try to fix it. ☐

Faith likes to play relaxing tunes. ☐

The greedy girls demanded new bikes. ☐

treat	treated	mistreated	☐
mast	dismast	dismasted	☐
tract	extract	extracted	☐
pain	painless	painlessly	☐
drink	drinkable	undrinkable	☐

The nasty boy mistreated his pet snail. ☐

They treated the dirty water to make it drinkable. ☐

The sailing boat was dismasted in the squall. ☐

Luke's rotten teeth were painlessly extracted. ☐

My dad's home-made wine is undrinkable. ☐

> old, cold, hold, both, most, were, once, only

I have only once got up at ___ to watch the sun rise.

    hold   most   dawn

Grace and Bruce both ___ to Greece last year.

    swam   walked   flew

If your hands are cold, hold them near the ___.

    fridge   flames   frames

Most of my friends were chewing ___.

    sludge   gunge   gum

FLUENCY READING

☐ Pass: 10 sec. ☆ Bonus: 8 sec. ☆☆ Double Bonus: 6 sec.

Luke	batch	expand	point	☐ ☆ ☆
fudge	unstuck	night	smoke	☐ ☆ ☆
eke	badge	fetch	often	☐ ☆ ☆
right	reset	failing	pitch	☐ ☆ ☆
puck	ridge	prefix	croak	☐ ☆ ☆
sight	exact	ditch	thankless	☐ ☆ ☆

Mastery Test

Any pupil who does not pass this test must go back to page 149. This is very important—a child who is struggling will not be learning. Contrary to what you would think, most children do not mind going back. It's better than getting things wrong.

If the pupil needs to go back, use a different coloured pencil for ticking the boxes.

Timed reading: 'Pass' mark is 15 seconds per line.

cue	slate	unsafe	maudlin	☐
boasting	crew	scope	useful	☐
redrawn	value	gripe	chewing	☐
tune	airless	sprayed	blew	☐

Reading accuracy: Pass mark is one mistake.

Do not prompt. You may allow the pupil to self correct, but you cannot say anything except "Try again".

Nate threw a few brass screws in the blue tin. ☐

Those new chimes send a chill down my spine. ☐

June helped me plant a few yew trees from Kew Gardens. ☐

If Lew will sharpen the blade of his knife, Dawn will cut the twine. ☐

The Rocky Shore.

Mark was proud to have a real job, but he was afraid, too. Mark was now the port lookout and he could just see over the rail. As far as he could see, there was only water. The cold spray hurt his skin and he had to squint to see in the driving rain. The rusty old trawler creaked and groaned as it pounded into the waves. Mark wished he was back in Bart's shack with Vern and Froid. He wished he was with Hank, the hunch-backed horse, who was a real mate, or with Jake, the fake snake, in his rusty old junk cars. At a pinch, even Mike, the loan shark, would do. Maybe he should have changed into a witch at the church by the strange bridge, where Smudge, the batty cat with a flat cap, lived. But it was no good wishing that he had not gone fishing. He hoped that Neal had a good home to take him to.

Mark was almost dreaming when he saw some lights. He yelled to Neal, the real seal, who came running over as fast as his flippers would go. "Look over there!" Mark pointed to the lights. Neal took out his spy-glass and looked at the lights. "Why, that is land over there. If the wind forces us on to the rocks, this rusty old trawler is done. And so are we." Neal told Maud and she stopped crying right away. Maud told Nate, the first mate, who gave up trying to light his pipe and threw it over the rail. They looked at the lights and at last Nate said, "That must be the rocky shore of Bangalore.

If we can't get more speed out of this old tub, it will smash on those rocks."

Maud said, "We need more steam if we are to get away from the rocky shore. Someone must go and help Sue, the gruesome stoker. She must have help shovelling coal into the boiler." But no one wanted to go below. No one wanted to be trapped in the boiler room when the trawler hit the rocks.

Maud said, "I must stay by the wheel and steer this ship, so I cannot go below." Nate, the first mate, said, "I must stay and bark at the crew, so I cannot go down to the boiler room." Neal, the real seal, said, "I cannot shovel coal because I cannot hold a shovel in my flippers."

So at last Mark said, "There is no point in looking out because we know exactly what is there. I will go below and help Sue shovel coal."

Do you think the trawler will hit the rocks?

Do you think that Mark will get dirty again?

You will find out when you start the next book!